ANATOLE DAUMAN
Pictures of a Producer

D1479379

Anatole Dauman
PICTURES OF A PRODUCER

JACQUES GERBER

TRANSLATED BY
PAUL WILLEMEN

BFI Publishing

Published in 1992 by the
British Film Institute
21 Stephen Street
London W1P 1PL

Gift 5-94

English edition copyright © British Film Institute 1992

Original French edition © Editions du Centre Georges
Pompidou, Paris 1989   no d'éditeur: 664
(ISBN of French edition 2 85850 522 5)

PN
1998.3
.D38
A3
1992

British Library Cataloguing in Publication Data
Gerber, Jacques
Anatole Dauman: Pictures of a Producer.

I. Title 791.430232092
ISBN 0 85170 290 2

Cover: Geoff Wiggins

Typeset in Plantin and Courier by
Discript, London
and printed by
The Trinity Press, Worcester

CONTENTS

ACKNOWLEDGMENTS

I gratefully acknowledge the assistance provided by the staff of Argos Films: Françoise Bazannery, Françoise Dubocq, Naomi Harris, Jenny Scheubeck, Ephrem Paraiso, Thierry Pillon, Jacques Réra, Sygmunt Rybarski, André Valio and especially Nadia Maschino, Mireille Mirowski and Jean-Noël Félix.

I would also like to thank Pascale Dauman, Sylvie Pras, Dominique Ruspoli, Jean Cayrol, Jean-Luc Godard, Jean-Loup Passek, Jean-Louis Pays, Camille Scalabre.

Anabela Abreu Pais, 'Anna', Anatole Dauman's chef, will not be forgotten for her familial meals and neither will Pedro Manuel Pereira Joaquim, occasional photographer and major-domo.

As for Anatole Dauman, I am now letting him go to 'the end of the world'. . . .

Jacques Gerber

[The French edition of this book, produced with the help of Noëlle de Chambrun, was conceived as part of the programme devoted to Anatole Dauman by the Centre Georges Pompidou from 31 May to 16 October 1989, curated by the Cinema Advisor, Jean-Loup Passek, assisted by Sylvie Pras.]

Photographic credits

ROAD MOVIES

F I L M P R O D U K T I O N   G m b H

Potsdamer Straße 199 · 1000 Berlin 30 · Telefon (030) 216 80 11

HRB 10595 Amtsgericht Berlin Charlottenburg · Geschäftsführer: Wim Wenders

M. Anatole Dauman
4 rue Edouard Nortier
92200 Neuilly sur Seine

Berlin 19.7.86

Dear Anatole,

Surely, an angel passed late last night when, having
lost all hope of ever being able to hold them in
our hands, we finally signed our contracts. And
still, early this morning in the plane, it was a
great pleasure to read them again: something makes
itself felt in them that has nothing to do either
with money or with the financial conditions of our
joint project, nor even with co-production arrange-
ments. Something that bears witness to a spirit and
a respect which you yourself last night called 'the
love of cinema'. I totally agree and I am proud of
that definition. But what a responsibility! I can
only hope that I will be capable of making a film
worthy of that contract!

   If only your nice lawyer were able to propose (and
then to get signed) such an agreement with my
guardian angel.

   Hochachtungsvoll

                    und mit herzlichsten Grüssen,

                              Wim Wenders

PREFACE

Anatole Dauman is my friend and my supporter. These have not always been easy roles to play. He has been steadfast.

I once made a speech to a group of New York theatre people about the man in the American theatre I most esteem, Harold Clurman. He'd directed many plays and some of them had been great successes. He'd also written the best criticisms in our time. I thought about my subject carefully and tried to isolate what it was about Harold I admired most. In the end what I said was that Harold's greatest achievement was not any of the productions he'd done but himself, the man himself. I feel something of that kind about Anatole. I haven't seen most of the films he's produced and I can't say precisely what he's contributed to any of them but they all seem to have one quality in common, an aspiration to be works of art. In Anatole's case too, and perhaps more important than the films he's produced, is the man himself, what he is and what he stands for.

Months ago, a close friend of mine, the critic Michel Ciment, recommended that I talk about the film I'm planning to Anatole. That started our friendship. The first thing I discovered about him was that he has a mind. He is actually interesting to talk with. He has the ambivalence and the mystery of an artist. He says what you don't anticipate on any given subject, and rarely what you expect him to say – the blight on the conversation of most people on the West Coast of the United States. Their reactions tend to be predictable.

Dauman often expressed ideas that made me question myself. I found that pleasurable as well as spurring. Stimulated by our table talk, I began to look forward to our meals together. He took me to art galleries, led me to working painters, introduced me to restaurants I didn't know existed. The main item on our bill of fare was conversation.

Anatole did not have a great deal to say about our screenplay but what he did say was of a conceptual and thematic nature. He didn't bully me with trifles or specifics. He left solutions to my son, Chris, and to me. When it came to casting, which because of my regard for him and his production staff I decided to do entirely in Europe, Anatole was sensitive and helpful. I felt no pressure from him to squeeze 'names' into my cast for commercial reasons. I found my own actors; he helped me meet them and, later, secure them.

He's been generous about money. When I thought it necessary to make location-hunting trips, he quickly put up the wherewithal for me and my designers to go to Turkey and to Greece. Twice. When it became evident that we might have difficulties with the politicians of these countries concerning my request to operate within their borders and the trust I sought for my friendly intentions, a trust difficult to grant with my screenplay, Anatole shouldered the job. Knowledgeable about the inner workings of political power, whom to see, whom to enlist, whom to ask for help, he succeeded in influencing the politicians whose help I needed.

I have served ten years on the National Board of the Directors Guild of America, and played a role in certain deliberations dealing with the artistic rights of directors. There was one goal which, over those ten years, I have failed to bring closer to realisation, namely the most important way of protecting a director's artistic rights in his film. This is referred to in America as the right to the final cut. There has been a period in my film-making when my films prospered at the box office. During that period I had that right. Then I made some films I liked equally well and in some cases better but they did not do as well in the market-place. I no longer had final cut and have never regained it in America.

As soon as I began working seriously with Anatole on production, I asked him about final cut. He replied that it wasn't necessary to negotiate it in our contract. I had it. In France, he told me, film-makers have final cut as if by law. It is not questioned or qualified. The man who makes the film, makes the film. Integral to that is how he cuts it. No one can mess up a film except its director. I discovered that this was emblematic of Anatole's personal policy in film-making. His effort was to help the director achieve what he, the director, wanted to achieve. *Help*, that is the key word. And to achieve what the *director* wants to achieve, not what the investors hope he will achieve.

What involves this man with a film project is less the script and the budget and never, in my experience, opportunities to possibly include stars. It is this feeling for the artistic worth of the film and the attraction the theme and subject have for him. He responds instinctively to an offer of involvement and I believe the judgment he makes is whether the work of the director on that screenplay might result in something that can aspire to the name of art, and, therefore, only therefore, be worth his time and effort. This exemplifies the difference between this man and most producers I've worked with in the United States. Particularly now, budget and star mean everything to them. They are basically public relations people, lawyers and book-keepers.

I'm fond of Anatole personally, but the basic allegiance I have to him is as a result of his attitude toward film-making. We are both interested in the struggle to make, if we possibly can, a film that is personal, unique and related to the problems of the world and of mankind. For this cause he will help a film-maker and become his producer, even when it is difficult, as it often is with the most worthy films, to raise the financing for their production.

Look at the list of films he has produced – you will find them on the pages that follow. Can you single out one of them that would have been made by a producer in Hollywood? Neither can I. Still Anatole made them, which is to say he helped a director make them, as the director wishes them to be. It is a question of one friend helping another to make the film they both want to make. A bond of mutual interest is developed and this has been developed between Anatole and me. It is also a bond of friendship. Anatole has the patience of a friend, he has the devotion of a friend and he has the concern of a friend. I hereby return that concern, that friendship and that devotion.

Elia Kazan
14 March 1989

'Will the producer be saved from perdition to figure in the last images of the Wenders world . . . ?' – Anatole Dauman, photographed by Chris Marker

THE OWL OF MINERVA

I was born many times, it seems, and I never know which event installed me more solidly in this life: my adoption by Germany in 1956, Argos' owl taking wing from my first offices on the Champs-Élysées in 1949, or the break with my uncle Adolphe Dauman in 1942.

Germany took an interest in my case when it discovered a film I had produced about the death camps, *Nuit et brouillard* by Alain Resnais. Because of the consideration it gave me on that occasion, I was able to achieve a solid and lasting cinematographic foothold in Franco-German co-production. Thanks to Germany, I have experienced strange paradoxes such as my entry into the imposing signified of my friend Volker Schlöndorff; me, a Freudian through and through with a taste for the art of the cinema that proscribes any manipulation of what is called reasoning reason. In the same way, I subscribed to the angelic romanticism of the creature of the clouds (Wim Wenders) in spite of the fairly dominant character in my career of an erotic tendency flattered by Poland and Japan.

In 1949, founded by Philippe Lifchitz and myself, my modest enterprise for the production, rental and world distribution of short films, Argos Films, settled into a vast room with a rear window located above the Ermitage cinema at 72, avenue des Champs-Élysées. The short-term lease, frequently renewed, was bitterly negotiated with Champs-Élysées Real Estates. A part-time secretary and an occasional accountant lent their services to our strongly personalised structure. In order to gain access to their office, the two founders of Argos Films had to sneak by the long queues of spectators anxious to partake of the pleasures of the big screen in the Ermitage.

The idea came to us of sharing the rent and the charges and accommodating a sub-tenant by erecting a glazed partition in the middle of our large office. A small plump man appeared in our space. A pre-war producer with a busy tongue and full of stories, Henri Ullmann[1] arose again to professional life after four years of action in the Resistance where, among other things, he directed the French forces which had been regrouped on the north face of the Vercors range. His life as a producer had been hazardous, marked by moments of splendour and of misery bearing the names of films. Through the partition, I could see him busily gesturing, seized by the desire to remake himself while feverishly preparing a remake of *La nuit est à nous* (Dir. Henri Roussell, 1929), a big hit of the early talkies. To forget his troubles he used to eat a pheasant ragout at Luigi's, because he wasn't entirely without means. His film portfolio included Abel Gance's

Lucrèce Borgia. Whenever his treasury was in a bit of a predicament, Ullmann had an infallible solution: he would adopt an air of craftiness and say, 'I'm going to put my whore into circulation again.' The notorious shot of Edwige Feuillère, naked, stretched out in her bath, would keep the wolf from the door, even though the projectionists tended to snip bits out of the film and kept for themselves the crucial part of the mythical images where Woman became Truth. Henri Ullmann revealed to me the glories and the disappointments of the cinema. Did he really have an amorously intimate dinner with Colette Darfeuil and Ginette Leclerc,[2] a story he enjoyed telling when he wanted to astound us? Anyway, every Saturday afternoon without fail he would take down the flag from above his desk and go to the tomb of the unknown soldier at the Arc de Triomphe to kindle the flame, because he was as big a patriot as he was a ladies' man.

I had to do without the benefits of a university education when launching myself into the roulette game the post-war producers were playing. My meagre studies at the Lycée Pasteur in Neuilly had been relieved by the proximity of some great men I observed with all the curiosity of an amateur entomologist. Jean-Paul Sartre, wearing a shaggy coat that fell down to the ground, would embark on long talks with his students while drawing on his pipe. That liberty drew the frowning attention of Philippe Van Tieghem who taught at the Lycée before he became a professor at the Sorbonne. A specialist in romanticism and the son of the famous expert in comparative literature, Van Tieghem considered it uncouth to carry on with one's students in the way that Sartre did in the back room of the café Le Sabot Bleu in Neuilly. The formality of Van Tieghem, the lord of knowledge, didn't detract in the least from his personal warmth which I could fully appreciate when I was lucky enough to have him as a father-in-law.

One of the most fruitful lessons at the Lycée Pasteur was dispensed by the magazine of the philosophy students, the *Trait d'union*, which counted both Chris Marker and Jacques Besse[3] among its contributors. That is where I was able to read the text of *Situations*, which Sartre wanted his students to read first. Its memorable pages on Dos Passos ended with this judgment: 'God is not an artist; neither is François Mauriac.' Sartre excoriated Mauriac's narrative structure, which was founded on identification with the characters, and instead celebrated the fragmented objectivity of Dos Passos, the collage technique, the recourse to 'newsreels' and to the 'camera eye'. All that was very stimulating for a student such as I, but was in no way sufficient to guarantee my accession to the high distinction of the baccalauréat, which the war then came to remove from my, if truth be told, rather doubtful aspirations.

Nevertheless, the Resistance provided a remedy for the inconveniences that might have ensued from that timidity in the face of the academic process. I sat my baccalauréat in rather troubled circumstances aggravated by a zero in German inflicted by an examiner who had been informed that my numerous absences were due to my early activities in the Resistance. I had in fact started to organise the clandestine printing press Libération Sud in Nice. After I had joined the Georges France 31 network, I was arrested and then I escaped. I rose in rank, and by the end of the war I had been invested with the kind of authority that made it incumbent on me to write officially to the vice-chancellor of the academy of Aix-en-Provence to request from him a report on the acts of collaboration he had been able to ascertain within the rector's office. Instead of the expected indictment I received a charming letter addressing me as 'Dear Lieutenant' but without a word about the investigations he was supposed to have conducted into the dossiers of the collaborators. The last sentences of the letter concerned me personally and went something like this: 'I availed myself of the opportunity to peruse with interest your academic records which had been forwarded to this office. I was surprised to find that you had been the victim of circumstances beyond your control and of spiteful treatment by one of the functionaries currently removed from the administration. I would like to take this opportunity to restore you to your rights and to grant you the just rewards of your academic merits by awarding you immediately, and with my compliments, the degree of the baccalauréat.'

Overjoyed by this dramatic turn of events which opened before me the way into the great French University at the dawn of the national renewal, I must admit that I did not insist that the vice-chancellor hand over a more incriminating report on the secret dossiers pertaining to the sad business of collaboration in his academy.

But when, really, was I born to the implacable hardness of life? As I grew older in my producer's profession, I noticed that all my inclinations impelled me towards apparently contradictory systems. For instance, my borrowed Germanness clashes with my strictly pataphysical[4] turn of mind. For the screen I produce 'mouthfuls of poison',[5] phantasms, maleficences that make the censors' hairs stand on end, while my life is played out in the driest possible registers. A servant of so-called literary cinema, I have no culture other than a kind of pretend culture, laboriously acquired and badly irrigated because of the bitter necessities of business life. But above all, I experience the curious feeling of having been prey to the temptation of fratricide (when I was younger), then of parricide when travelling alongside great directors desperately fleeing from their creation or impatiently bent on dragging me into a double death leap. I developed a taste for dedicating myself to the infernal talent of others, something which is usually resisted, in the products of a proper education, by the sense of self-sufficiency that families seek to foster in their dearest offspring. However, from my family, a vast Russian-Polish drift that came to a halt in Bälty in Romania, then in Warsaw, Nice and Paris according to the fluctuations of the bourgeoisie's fortunes in the jazz age, I really only retain the edifying impact of one single event: the break with my uncle Adolphe one day in 1942 on the pavement of the Promenade des Anglais in Nice.

My uncle Adolphe Dauman was the eldest and the most brilliant of four industrial brothers (one of them being my father) who had founded in Poland a fairly large factory producing alcohols with varied technical and commercial applications. Coquettishly or as a sly way of exploiting the intemperance of the large workforce, uncle Adolphe assisted by my father added a vodka distillery to the business under the label 'Daumana Vodka'. Uncle Adolphe was an impressively elegant character, wearing a monocle, an opera-hat and a frock-coat in the most everyday of circumstances, as when he went on inspection tours in the villages where his factory workers lived. Well endowed by nature, a model of familial perfection, he radiated a kind of powerful universality that left profound traces in the memories of those who had been exposed to the shock of his presence.

One of my collaborators at Argos, Sygmunt Rybarski, formerly the director of production at the Polish government's documentary studios (and exemplary production manager of *Nuit et brouillard*), perfectly remembers his early childhood days in Ostrowiec when he and his father greeted the passing carriage ferrying uncle Adolphe among the buildings of the Dauman factory. An immense moustache, at times caressed by the handle of his cane or interfering with the sun-bonnets of elegant ladies, subjugated the population. One day when I was doing business with an Australian lawyer in the Brasserie Lorraine, to my astonishment he informed me that his father, a Polish émigré, had known uncle Adolphe in identical circumstances. A bottle of vodka with his likeness on the label had been carefully preserved on the big farm in the bush of New South Wales where that Polish-Australian family now lived. Uncle Adolphe was a true cosmopolitan. That prodigious character was a converted Jew. However, his borrowed faith remained completely unnoticeable throughout the happy years when the four brothers Dauman, assisted by their brother-in-law Fidler (a Russian, a decorator, always wearing gaiters), held the high ground in the business world from Bessarabia to the suburbs of Warsaw, and during their intermittent Mediterranean holidays.

Having retired to the heights of Cimiez in Nice during the occupation, uncle Adolphe was seized by an infinitely more lively and profound interest in Catholicism under the influence of a priest who was very well known in the Polish community and who bore the beautiful name of Merda. As the Vichy police tightened its stranglehold on the Jews who had sought refuge in the free French zone, uncle Adolphe and Father Merda became inseparable. Paul Fabian, one of my friends from the Resistance who had Polish nationality, was seriously threatened by the racial persecutions and it fell to me to try and obtain for him a false certificate of baptism. It occurred to me to ask this favour of uncle Adolphe who was so well in with the church. We met well away from indiscreet ears on the Promenade des Anglais and he said this to me: 'My dear Anatole, do you think that I converted to Christianity purely and simply because it was convenient to do so? I want you to know that I found in that religion principles which I hold above any matters of mere convenience. I observe them rigorously. They are God's commandments and among them is this one: thou shalt not lie. I would like to help your friend but I cannot, in the eyes of Father Merda, make myself an accomplice of an outright lie. A Jew is a Jew. If he does not want to convert himself, that means he wants to be a Jew. That is how Father Merda will see it.' My break with uncle Adolphe was immediate and total. But shortly after that pitiless discourse of absolute truth triumphant, he was so frightened by the big roundup of foreign Jews organised by Laval in the so-called free zone that he fell down dead, struck by a heart attack. Uncle Adolphe died of being a Jew. He received a nice funeral in the cathedral, but truth had finally triumphed over lies.

Emerging from the war and from that familial disappointment, I started my career in the cinema with daily joys and nightly pleasures which have long since vanished from my life. During the day, the lively way I went about my work in the offices of Argos Films owed much to the charming company of my associate Philippe Lifchitz. My dear Philippe was a sprightly character who cultivated English gentlemanly customs. Often he deprived me of his presence in order to go and exercise on the tennis courts his remarkable talents as a top seeded player. In the afternoon, his demons would drive him into nearby dance halls in quest of some adventure. He would return, if at all, around the time that I would be closing the office, wearing a debonair smile. He was an inveterate worshipper of holidays as an institution. Every day he would fire off his witty repartee over cups of tea and multiply his vast range of hobbies, which extended our professional horizons to exotic shores. One day, at the very end of July, while we were in the middle of our preparations for a film, he communicated to me by letter his desire for sun, sea and pure air. We separated after ten years which had turned me into an anglophile.

The long and industrious days in the Argos office often ended with nocturnal excursions to cabarets such as La Rose Noire or La Rose Rouge, Chez Agnès Capri, La Fontaine de Grenelle, to the small Left Bank theatres, the cinémathèque of the rue Messine and the cellar of Milord l'Arsouille. Many people with lively minds and of pleasant company, free from any taint of vulgarity, liked meeting up in the cabarets of Saint-Germain-des-Prés. Among them was the fortune-teller Virel, the co-author with Prévert and André Verdet of *Le Cheval de Troie*.[6] He introduced an air of mystery with his poetic improvisations and tarot readings. I remember one day when he told the fortune of some friends of mine who had come to dinner. He didn't know that a few yards away from him, by the foot of a lampstand, a thermometer had been hidden. Suddenly, there was a noise in that part of the room. Virel jumped up and, flushed with embarrassment, stuttered: 'I didn't mean to do that.' The thermometer had been reduced to a heap of powdered glass at the foot of the lampstand. On another occasion I introduced him to Myriam Bru whose youthful beauty had just been consecrated Miss Côte d'Azur. While they were out walking one night in the Tuileries gardens, Virel went off and straddled the back of a bronze lion. 'Yes, my dear Anatole,' she later assured me, 'Virel climbed onto the lion and the lion wagged his tail. I'll swear to it.' She had me convinced. Queneau's spirit was also out and about at that time. The Grenier-Hussenot company and Yves Robert's theatre group were making a strong impression. Jacques Fabbri performed poetic compositions on stage which enchanted everyone.[7] All those things were new but hardly reasonable. They were new things inspired by traditions such as that of Jarry and Alphonse Allais,[8] a tradition that had broken with the solid good sense of the bourgeois theatre. I was able to breathe and it was fun.

The opening of the night-club La Rose Noire was celebrated by the journalists of *Samedi Soir* and of *France-Dimanche*. Maurice Chevalier danced with Michel de Ré's[9] first wife. She was so pregnant she looked about to burst. Jean-Paul Sartre was there too. It is at La Rose Noire that I met Nico Papatakis.[10] He was happy to be the bouncer while his companion, Mireille, staged shows in the back room. From one day to the next, people flocked to La Rose Noire, but the takings didn't get to the organisers, such as Mireille and a few others. So it became necessary to find another site and that was La Rose Rouge where Nico, this time as the boss, and Mireille as the manageress took charge. As part of the show at La Rose Rouge there was a short film produced and directed off the cuff by Henri Gruel, *Martin et Gaston*. I liked that animated film made with paper cut-outs very much. As soon as it had been given a respectable identity under the stewardship of the Centre national de la cinématographie, I blew it up to 35mm for commercial exhibition. After the big success of *Martin et Gaston* I asked Gruel to make another animated film using the same technique: that was *Le Voyage de Badabou*. Armed in one hand with *Badabou* and with Jacques Baratier's *Paris, la nuit* in the other, I decided to attack the big film prizes. My sights were set on the Louis Delluc Prize, which at that time was to cinema what the Goncourt was to literature. Unfortunately, its rules precluded giving the prize to a short film. I conducted such a ferocious campaign on behalf of *Paris, la nuit* that the jury was so unsettled that René Clair had to wait until the third voting round before he could get his laurels. Henri Jeanson, who was the president of the jury, hadn't felt comfortable defending René Clair's film against the assault from *Paris, la nuit*. After all, he was giving the prize to an in-house author working for the same employer as himself, Cinédis, one of the most important outfits of the period. The next day Jeanson came into my office and shouted: 'Do you want me to give the Lumière Prize to *Paris, la nuit*?'

'No, thanks,' I replied, 'I'd prefer you to give that to the odds on favourite, Gruel's film, *Badabou*.'

'Never mind,' Jeanson answered, 'I am going to set up a special prize for animated films, the Émile Cohl Prize.[11] You'll get that for *Badabou* and then we can give the Lumière Prize to *Paris, la nuit*, which is what I want to do.'[12] No sooner said than done. I humbly accepted the wise distribution of prizes orchestrated by Jeanson. I got both prizes. I sold the rights for *Badabou* to be released on the same bill as René Clément's *Gervaise*, which was a tremendous success. As for *Paris, la nuit*, Cousteau[13] had loved the film and he asked me to sell it, very dearly, to Rank, who distributed *Le Monde du silence* which was to receive the Palme d'Or in Cannes.

My business was taking off and already I was slipping into the terrain staked out by Robert Bresson's prodigious achievement, *Le Journal d'un curé de campagne* (1951): directors who wanted to base their films on literary texts. When I went to see Bresson's film, I obviously went to see one scene in particular: the priest's death. But I fell under the spell of this extraordinary marriage between literature and the image. The presence of a great text, far from contravening the specificity of the cinema, broke with the way the soundtrack had been taken over by the continuous rumble of the scriptwriters' well-oiled dialogues. Another example of this indispensable step forward proved equally revelatory: Jean Cocteau's *Les Parents terribles*, with tragedy, cloaked in bourgeois garb, insinuating itself, quietly developing and eventually being unleashed. My first feature, *Le Rideau cramoisi* by Alexandre Astruc, had stemmed from my curiosity about 'crimes of love'. There, to be honest, the literary dimension was used to hide the modesty of production resources: shooting with a voice-over allowed me to save the expense of shooting with direct sound. But for *Watteau* I was so certain it was the right thing to do that I imposed the choice of Ribemont-Dessaignes, the dadaist poet, on the director. To me, Ribemont was a legendary figure, even though only a few initiates knew his name. I was proud to be able to borrow some of his talent for my short film. From then on, I wanted to cut public sensibilities to the quick. That's how the 'literary' bias of the good ship Argos came about, guided by the owl of Minerva, or in Hegel's terms, Thought.

Why Argos, a name evoking the thousand eyes of a monster? I can't remember. On the other hand, the owl, Argos' emblem, can be found inscribed on the tablets of history. Prior to my turning towards the cinema, I had wanted to become a publisher of art books. I had thought of calling the publishing house The Owl of Mercury. The confusion in my autodidact's mind between Mercury (Commerce) and Minerva (Thought) was heartily approved of by my surrealist friend Henri Pastoureau. He considered it to be an irrational and therefore a poetic association. It is through Henri Pastoureau that I came to know the de Sade commentator, Gilbert Lely, and the painter Labisse whom we irreverently called Lapisse because of his paintings. Personally, I have no animistic veneration for the owl whatsoever. I subscribe to the trappings of that image only because of the profound sympathy my friend Chris Marker has for that animal.

Such were the beginnings of the Argos enterprise up to the point where it became involved in the so-called literary cinema: a cinema not of literary adaptations but of cineastes who invent an exceptional relation between the text and the images. Argos's authors, to whom I owe the memories that will follow, succeed in this because they borrow literature from nobody but themselves: they are writers.

NOTES

1. The producer Henri Ullmann, known also as Henri Vendresse, produced *L'École des contribuables*, R. Guissart (1934); *Dédé*, R. Guissart (1934); *Fédora*, L. Gasnier (1934); *Compartiment de dames seules*, Christian-Jaque (1934); *La Famille Pont-Biquet*, Christian-Jaque (1935); *Lucrèce Borgia*, A. Gance (1935); *On ne roule pas Antoinette*, P. Madeux (1936); *Oeil-de-lynx, détective*, P.J. Ducis (1936); *Au soleil de Marseille*, P.J. Ducis (1937); *Le Porte-veine*, A. Berthomieu (1937).

2. [Colette Darfeuil, born as Emma-Henriette Floquet in 1905 in Paris, was France's leading silent film vamp. She was said to have the most beautiful eyes in the French cinema and, from 1923 onwards, a screen presence that out-sizzled Clara Bow. Unfortunately, all too often her presence was the only saving grace of the films in which she appeared, except perhaps for *L'éternelle idole* (Guido Brignone, 1930), *La fin du monde* (Abel Gance, 1931), *Mirages de Paris* (Fedor Ozep, 1932), *Le truc brésilien* (Cavalcanti, 1933), *La maison*

dans la dune (P. Billon, 1933), *Minuit Place Pigalle* (Richebé, 1934, in which she appeared together with Ginette Leclerc), *Mon Cœur t'appelle* (Carmine Gallone, 1934), *La Chanson du souvenir* (D. Sirk, 1936), *Le Patriote* (M. Tourneur, 1938), *L'Avion de minuit* (D. Kirsanoff, 1938), *Untel Père et fils* (J. Duvivier, 1940). She also provided the script for *Voici Dimanche* (Weill, 1930).

Ginette Leclerc, born in 1912 in Paris as Geneviève Manut. Started as a model for erotic postcards and became the best known vamp of the thirties and forties, mostly cast as a 'loose woman'. She remained active in the cinema and on the stage until the mid-seventies and was said to have been murdered more times on screen than any woman in the French cinema. She also had a career as a singer. Her most impressive role was in H.G. Clouzot's *Le Corbeau* (1943). Films include: *La dame de chez Maxim's* (Korda, 1933), *Ciboulette* (Autant-Lara, 1933), *Cette vieille canaille* (Litvak, 1933), *Toto* (M. Tourneur, 1934), *Le compartiment des dames seules* (Christian-Jaque, 1934), *L'Homme de nulle part* (P. Chenal, 1937, her real breakthrough film), *La femme du boulanger* (M. Pagnol, 1938), *Prison sans barres* (L. Moguy, 1938), *Louise* (Abel Gance, 1938), *L'Empreinte du dieu* (L. Moguy, 1940), *Fièvres* (J. Delannoy, 1941), *Le Val d'enfer* (M. Tourneur, 1943), *Le dernier sou* (A. Cayatte, 1944), *Un homme marche dans la ville* (M. Pagliero, 1949), *Le plaisir* (Max Ophuls, 1951), *Le cave se rebiffe* (J.P. Grangier, 1961), *Goto* (Walerian Borowczyk, 1968), *Le grand cérémonial* (A. Jolivet, 1968), *Le Bal du Comte d'Orgel* (Allégret, 1969), *Popsy pop* (J. Herman, 1970), *Les volets clos* (J.-C. Brialy, 1972), *Spermula* (E. Matton, 1975), *La barricade du point du jour* (Richon, 1977). Her memoirs were published as *Ma vie privée*.]

3. [Jacques Besse was a promising young musician. He provided the score for Resnais's short on *Van Gogh*. Almost immediately after Dauman hired him to do the music for *L'Affaire Manet*, he succumbed to a mental illness.]

4. [See note 6.]

5. 'A hefty mouthful of poison' was the title of André Breton's essay on the Argos Films production *Mina de Vanghel.*

6. [Jacques Prévert (1900–1977) was an extremely popular poet and scenarist, best known in the cinema for his many scripts, including Renoir's *Le crime de Monsieur Lange* (1935) and many collaborations with Marcel Carné (including *Drôle de drame, Quai des brumes, Le jour se lève, Les visiteurs du soir, Les enfants du paradis, Les portes de la nuit, La Marie du port*). He did a number of absurdist, rather surreal pieces in collaboration with André Verdet (who was often nicknamed André PréVerdet at the time), including this volume of poems first published in 1946. The title is a pun on the Trojan Horse and a horse ridden by or belonging to three people (the third collaborator was André Virel).]

7. [Jacques Fabbri's full name was Fabriciotti. Born in 1925 in Paris, he had a successful career as a theatre director and actor. His obtained his biggest success staging C. Santelli's *La Famille Arlequin* at the Vieux-Colombier in 1955, for which he received the Molière Prize. He also mounted the *Cabaret Rive Gauche* spectacle, which was performed at the Rose Rouge club. His appearances as a film actor included *Rendez-vous de Juillet* (1949), *Les femmes sont des anges* and *Destinées* (1953), *Crainquebille* (1954) and *Les grandes manœuvres* (1955).]

8. [Alfred Jarry (1873–1907) was an absurdist author best known for his creation of the Ubu figure. He invented pataphysics, 'the science of imaginary solutions'.

Alphonse Allais (1855–1905) was a popular humorist and a prolific author.]

9. [Theatre director and actor born in 1925 as Michel Galliéni; active in cabaret after World War II and eventually a film and television actor. In 1946 he formed the Thiaze Company and mounted productions of Ribemont-Dessaignes' *Le Serin muet* and H. Michaux' *Chaînes*. He staged Prévert's comic sketch *En Famille, Contes pour enfants pas sages* [*In the Family: Tales for Naughty Children*] at the Rose Rouge club in 1947. He acted in G. Hanoteau's successful television serial *Le Commandant X* and went on to produce and star in the comic private eye series *Les Dossiers de Jérôme Randax*. His many appearances as a screen actor included Michel Deville's *Ce soir ou jamais* (1961), Roger

Leenhardt's *Le Rendez-vous de minuit* (1962), Serge Bourguignon's *Les Dimanches de Ville d'Avray* (1962), Roger Vadim's *Le Vice et la vertu* (1963) and Albert Lamorisse's *Fifi la Plume* (1965).]

10. Nico Papatakis was of Greek origin. Having been a prince of the night, he became a cineaste. He made *Les Abysses* (1963); *Les Pâtres du désordre* (1968); *Gloria Mundi* (1975); *La Photo* (1987).

11. [Émile Cohl, a pseudonym for Émile Courtet, was a cartoonist and animation pioneer, author of numerous animated films using a variety of techniques since 1907. The prize awarded in his name is for excellence in animated cinema.]

12. In 1951.

13. [Jacques-Yves Cousteau is the celebrated French cineaste and oceanographer.]

THE MONA LISA

(The story of an obsession. Commentary by Boris Vian
for the short film *The Mona Lisa*, directed by Henri
Gruel in 1957. The text was written in twenty-four
hours. It was corrected by Anatole Dauman and Boris
Vian in two hours.)

And ever since she was born, that 450-year-old lady
has been provoking passions and crimes . . . to the
point that her exploiters have now discreetly put
her under surveillance . . .

In the crime world's jargon, that kind of an
informer is called 'a grass' or 'a stool-pigeon'.

The museum that lives off Mona Lisa's charms also
shows a great deal of striptease. For instance: the
Venus de Milo. Nevertheless, the bulk of the clients
come because of the place's most banal resident,
attracted by nothing more than her face.

This Turkish painter has been coming every morning
for twenty-seven years: he has copied that oblique
smile and the folded hands more than 200 times. More
than 150,000 copies spread throughout the world
offer themselves up to the admiration of all peoples.
The most advanced nations assess the power of their
artistic heritage in terms of Mona-horsepower.

Every day, on the commodity brokers' page,
journalists report on important movements in Mona
Lisa stocks. On foot, on horseback, in cars, the
Mona Lisa moves around the universe.

In Paris, every year 100,000 tourists pay their
money for a standard artistic turn-on. And many go
to look, ignoring what they have come to see: the
Mona Lisa; an abstract concept. How to escape from
the obsession?

The Mona Lisa is everywhere. She is branded into
innocent orange-skins. She gives the come-on for
Italian tourism. She slips into the corsets of decent
women.

Because she sells: cigars, aperitifs, projectors,
suspender belts, books . . .

A milk cow, fifteen race horses, one element of
the Saclay atomic reactor, all bear her name . . .

But why her? How did this moon-faced character,
smiling like a procuress, achieve such a reputation?

Who are you, Mona Lisa?

Leonardo da Vinci sees her coming in. Are you
coming for the cleaning lady's job? She doesn't

answer. She smiles.

Hmm, Leonardo thinks, at last one who keeps her mouth shut. And he takes her as a model.

Four years later, the painting is finished . . . and the mystery begins.

Mona, are you Isabelle d'Este?

It is a man, one critic assures us. Let us verify this hypothesis with an open mind and try out some becoming and typically male hair-dos. Well . . . There is no doubt . . . She is ugly, all right, but not ugly enough to be a man.

Let's go back to basics. What is the Mona Lisa?

An uncertain smile. Where does it come from?

Is it the raptured smile of a music nut enchanted by Leonardo's caressing tenor?

Is it the resigned smile of an inconsolable mother?

Is it the buddha-like smile of some Asian divinity?

Is it the charming smile of a barbarous Etruscan?

Answer: it is a satiated smile. Leonardo da Vinci, the famous inventor of cocktails, tried them out on his models. Of course we rejected the hypothesis that it is a professional smile. Besides, all sixteenth-century Italian women smiled obliquely. They even took lessons from the good master Angelo Firenzuola. Smile obliquely! . . . and fold your hands. The smile, the folded hands, that's the Mona Lisa in a nutshell.

That was the opinion of: Raphaël, Corot, Matisse, Soutine, Picasso and Léger.

The Mona Lisa obsesses the great and the good of this world.

And they all contribute their own commentary.

Elizabeth: enigmatic.

Bonaparte: The Sphinx of the West.

Cambronne:[1]

Dali: I am her. She is me.

George Sand: It isn't a person. It's an idée fixe.

Morse: Beep, beep, beep.

Michelet:[2] This canvas attracts, calls out, overwhelms, absorbs. Watch out.

Michelet's warning wasn't heeded. Luc Maspero, a young painter who lives in the attic of a moth-eaten hotel in old Saint-Denis, tries in vain to fix onto his canvas the smile that fascinated him. Lethal mistake. At the end of his tether, with a broken heart, Maspero jumps from the fourth floor.

Others are determined not to die without a fight.

On 22 August 1911, at seven in the morning, the house painter Vicenzo Perrugia slips into a deserted Louvre.

The voice of the court usher:
>   Twelve months in gaol
>   cousins accused as accomplices
>   to the station the lot of you.

The poet Guillaume Apollinaire is suspected of receiving stolen goods.

The voice of the court usher: Fatal mistake.

After the passively defensive stance of Perrugia, a direct attack.

On 30 December 1956, at 16.15, the waiter Hugo Unzaga Villegas suddenly throws a rock at Mona Lisa.

Unfortunately, he misses and only inflicts a wound of one square centimetre on her arm. He is charged with damaging an object of public utility.

The voice of the court usher: psychiatric hospital.

Like Jupiter, Mona Lisa first renders mad those she wants to destroy and at that game, she wins every time.

NOTES

1. [Pierre Cambronne (1770–1842) was a French general who, when summoned to surrender at Waterloo, allegedly replied 'Merde', i.e. 'shit'. That word has remained associated with his name ever since.]
2. [Jules Michelet (1798–1874) was France's most illustrious historian, also known for his stylistic sophistication.]

THE HORRIBLE, WEIRD AND INCREDIBLE ADVENTURE OF MISTER HEAD

(Commentary written by Eugène Ionesco for the short film *The Horrible, Weird and Incredible Adventure of Mister Head*, directed by Jan Lenica in 1959.)

The sun never rises at quite the same time. It always rises a little earlier than the day before, except in winter when it generally rises later.

That particular morning, the inhabitants of the city, alive, dead or suffering from insomnia, were still fast asleep.

Alas . . . the birds! the birds! the birds! the birds! . . . and the crowing cock. What a life! Courage . . .

As usual, I consulted my daily paper:

      - All quiet in the East!

      - In the West, all quiet.

      - Up there . . . still a bit chilly.

      - Down here . . . still as hot.

What a life! The mediocrity of life . . . had become unbearable. I could have been something other than an office clerk. I could have been someone like . . . Pirandello! . . . or Hannibal . . . Catherine the Great. Everything ought to be turned upside down!

The serpent of revolt bit me. Its venom spread throughout my veins.

Steady . . . steady . . . better resign ourselves . . . Time to go to the office.

Again, the serpent of revolt bit me . . . Its venom spread throughout my veins.

This life can't be real life . . . That's no reason to lose one's head.

      Let's at least save one soul.

      That wasn't the done thing!

      I was asked to leave the firm.

      It's the fault of this head. It thinks too much.

      Lousy head.

      - Take me back! said the head.

      - After all, one must have a head! . . . Too bad. One is stuck with the head one's got.

      Oh! to live on love! . . .

      She isn't in love with our head! the head suddenly told me.

      - But then what?

The serpent of revolt bit me! . . . its
venom spread throughout my veins.
'Happy love doesn't exist . . .'
I'd prefer them . . . roasted! . . .
A banquet! What if I went?
I choked . . . The serpent of revolt bit me. Its
venom spread throughout my veins . . . I was no
longer master of my head . . . It was awful . . .
I had been resigned to everything . . .
But not that lousy head . . .
The serpent of . . .
– Oh rage, oh despair!
– Lousy head . . . It's your fault!
– They'll never get me!
– You'll listen to reason . . .
– No.
– Yes.
– No.
– Yes.
We hammered some sense into the head.
And the head was tamed . . .
I became a model citizen, a citizen full of wisdom
and virtue. There are compensations . . . Honours
. . . The serpent of revolt no longer spreads its
venom throughout my veins. At last, a head like any
other. In fact, everyone's head.

MINA DE VANGHEL

Mina de Vanghel poses and resolves the problems of adapting literature to the screen in surprising ways. That must be said right away and quite clearly. Maurice Clavel has treated the story with a freedom which, overshadowed by the film's authority, the confidence of its style and the importance of its text, we wouldn't notice except by referring to the original text. Often directors retain only a pretext or a theme from a work, or transpose a plot and its characters from one time and place to another. Renoir, who did it with *Les Bas-Fonds*, is getting ready to do it again with *Premier Amour*[1] after having taken Mérimée for a coach ride. But the extraordinary interlacing of fidelity and transposition that makes up the fabric of Clavel's film is probably unprecedented. In fact, the commentary spoken by Michel Bouquet, which has such a great dramatic and psychological importance, retains but three or four of the sentences from the original story. Clavel has rewritten an imaginary text by Stendhal which is even more Stendhalian than Stendhal. The most knowledgeable expert wouldn't be able to tell the bits that come from the original. But this isn't done for novelty's sake: rather like Stendhal would have written it had he been Clavel's scenarist. It is a diabolical skill, giving freedom to the director while guaranteeing faithfulness . . . of and to the writer. It is also a freedom which no doubt is not in everyone's reach: it is difficult to see who but Clavel would be able to enjoy its benefits.

So many disturbances of the economy of Stendhal's narrative aren't gratuitous. It would of course be possible to dispute their necessity from the strict point of view of the film's logic. Clavel indeed more or less eliminated all sense of dramatic progression by pushing, from the outset, the relations between the characters to their paroxysm: Mina's romantic love, her jealousy, her decision to win by means of the most impudent of lies, all these contain from the start the seeds of the ensuing events, none of which can really come as a surprise after that. Nothing essential is added: things are only rendered more explicit up to the heroine's inevitable death. But this reconstruction of the narrative finds its overall justification if we admit that Clavel has sacrificed Stendhal to Mina

Odile Versois in Mina de Vanghel

and, in Mina, the novelistic to the romantic. In other words, the adaptation started exclusively, not from the plot but from a vision of that Stendhalian microcosm seen in terms of its principal component: German romanticism. I take pleasure from imagining that in some future classroom Maurice Clavel's film would in forty-five minutes teach more about that spiritual and literary movement than three months of literary appreciation courses. Besides, *Le Rideau cramoisi* is also there to allow comparisons to be made with French romanticism.

André Bazin
Cahiers du cinéma

NOTE

1. [Jean Renoir's unrealised project to film Ivan Turgenev's *First Love*.]

Argos Films
Société à Responsabilité Limitée Capital 500.000 frs
— R.C. Seine 354.277
35 rue Washington
Paris VIII
Tel.: BAL 14-32 — BAL 03-59

Paris 29 February 1960

Mademoiselle Arletty
31, rue Raynouard
Paris XVI

Mademoiselle,
    We would like to confirm the proposals we made to
you:
CLAUSE 1 We employ you to speak in French the
commentary written by Mr Jacques Prévert for a short
film directed by Mr Pierre Prévert entitled:
                    Paris La Belle
which you have already viewed.
CLAUSE II The recording will be on 2 March 1960.
CLAUSE III We will send you, after the recording,
i.e. on 2 March 1960, the fee of 750 N.F. (seven
hundred and fifty New Francs).
That payment will be made to the Société ANDRÉ

Pierre and Jacques Prévert, with Marcel Duhamel, filming Paris La belle

BERNHEIM, 55, avenue George V, with a crossed cheque made out to it and for which we will receive a valid receipt.

CLAUSE IV It is understood that in all publicity and on the credits of the film your name will be cited in the most prominent typeface and in the following manner:

commentary spoken by ARLETTY

We would like to ask you to confirm your agreement to the conditions set out in this letter by returning the enclosed copy duly signed after the handwritten notification 'Read and approved. Agreed' and having initialled the bottom of the first page.

Yours sincerely,

A. DAUMAN

FROM BARATIER TO VARDA

JACQUES BARATIER

My friend Jacques Baratier invested a lot of talent in his ever so merry, lacerated life but he didn't always put as much into his work. I regard *Désordre* (1949), the title of his first short, as a perfect definition of the man, as well as of the director and the producer (he often produced his own films). He took the word from a Dostoevsky quote proudly displayed before the credits of the film: 'Disorder is mostly no more than a secret desire for order and beauty.' The images, edited with a keen sense of the art of the unexpected, outline the life of Saint-Germain-des-Prés where people who would soon become famous bumped into each other on every street corner according to an itinerary that only Baratier's camera could have mapped out for them.

I first met Jacques at La Ponche, a café in Saint-Tropez. He was with Robert Auboyneau, who said he was the son of the admiral although he was only the nephew. Both were selling handwritten tickets on which they had scribbled a modest price for the preview of a film. In the name of the profession, the inland revenue and of SACEM[1] I duly lectured the two perverts for flagrantly violating the levy and tax systems governing cinematic exhibition. With a disarming smile, Jacques countered my censoriousness by pointing out that he had a right to his personal whims. Much later, I acquired joint possession of the negative and the copyright of *Désordre*. This piece of entertainment found its way into a programme of short films I put together with my friend Armand Tallier and which did good business at the Ursulines for many months. Twenty years later, Jacques and I embarked on a new *Désordre* that would run for an hour and twenty minutes. That was *Le désordre a vingt ans*. The interweaving of the present and the past threw up, amongst other silhouettes, Juliette Gréco. On some piece of waste land, she was singing 'Si tu t'imagines' out of synch (the sound had been dubbed) to Raymond Queneau and Marcello Pagliero, prostrated before her black trousers. In the next shot, the waste land had become the Monoprix of the rue de Rennes, and Juliette, sporting a somewhat shorter nose, was walking amongst the crowd of customers. One evening, in order to brighten up the lacklustre lights of Saint-Germain-des-Prés, we rented the first floor of the Flore for the premiere. Boubal, the proprietor of the establishment, a melancholically smiling Amphitryon, was at the festivities. In between the two *Désordre* films, my encounters with Baratier bear the proud-sounding titles: *Paris, la nuit* in 1956, *Èves futures* in 1964 . . . But after those splendiferous times, a trap was

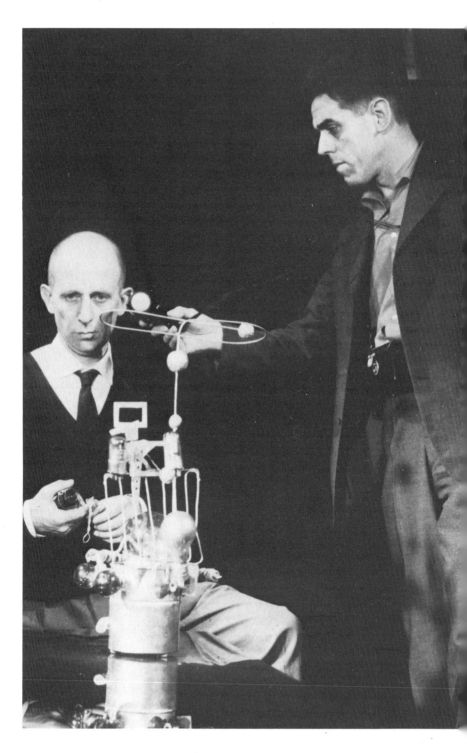

Jacques Baratier (left) *with the cinematographer Raoul Coutard*

about to be sprung on me.

Shooting in an intermittent and rather unpremeditated manner, Baratier was glad to have a friend who was a producer. But I was on my guard, knowing that the surprises he would spring on himself and on others compelled me to be cautious. I had accepted the idea for his short film *Piège* on the explicit condition that, as writer-director, he would obey the rules we would agree by mutual consent. His extreme sensitiveness and volatile moods made him an exquisite companion but a flighty collaborator who would take great offence at the most innocuous of suggestions. I wanted to hold him to a firm schedule as protection against the hazards of an unfocused inspiration and erratic directing. I asked him to sign a budget drawn up with collaborators of his choice, well known for their professionalism. Our agreement stipulated that the shoot couldn't exceed two weeks and the budget was solemnly assigned a ceiling of 103,000F. In this way I hoped to have fixed a firm framework enabling me to take a reasonable financial risk. But the film was called *Piège* (*Trap*) . . . . Wasn't that enough of a warning? The starring role was given to Bernadette Lafont for her comeback after a long interruption to her career during which she had set herself up in the country

Bernadette Lafont, Jean-Baptiste Thierrée and Bulle Ogier in Piège

Bulle Ogier in Piège

with a family and three children. She had, however, retained a distinct taste for the boards and the greasepaint. Baratier had found a choice partner for her: Bulle Ogier.

Shooting started in Neuilly in a villa slated for demolition where the director could indulge in all the refurbishing and dismantling he fancied. The evening before the last day of shooting, according to the schedule we had established, I went to the location to say goodbye to the crew and the actors. Baratier welcomed me on the set with the words: 'Anatole, you're a lucky devil because I've decided to give you a feature film for very little money. One more week and I'll give you a masterpiece!' On hearing that promise, my blood froze. Although I knew in advance that it would be useless, I waved our duly signed agreement in his face and declared: 'Edit your film with the material you have. I'm stopping the shoot the day after tomorrow.' Unbothered by his signature, our artist turned to his

Jacques Baratier filming La Poupée

collaborators and proposed that they defer their salaries in order to help finance the extra week of shooting he wanted. He didn't convince anyone, not even Bernadette Lafont even though she was keen on re-establishing her cinematic presence. As I didn't relish the idea of having to deal with an improvised co-operative, I decided to resolve the situation by allowing Baratier a few days extra. That compromise meant that the film wouldn't be as long as the envisaged masterpiece but would have the running time of about two short films.

I dearly wish I had paid more attention to the script our friend Baratier had concocted with the help of Jacques Tati! Arsène, a disturbed as well as a disturbing man, buys traps and fills his house with them. Will the burglars come? Tired of waiting for them, Arsène goes to the Petite-Roquette prison and gives his address to two female delinquents who have just been freed. Tendering them his card, he whispers: 'A sumptuous villa . . .', believing he has found his victims. One night later, he impotently witnesses the progress of his opponents, in the ravishing shapes of Bulle and Bernadette, as they circumvent all his traps and turn them against him . . .

Let there be no doubt: Arsène, that was me! In the middle of the fire that in the end consumes the scene of the crime, the female duo standing in for the director dance for joy on the ashes of the contract which I had been imprudent enough to sign with him.

I didn't renege on my friendship for Baratier, whose scintillating cinematic grace provided me with marvellous memories: *Cité du Midi*, *Métier de danseur*, *Paris, la nuit*, *Èves futures*, *Eden Miseria*. I can still see the scenes of *Cité du Midi*, shot well before the New Wave in a gym in Clichy. Michel Simon commented in a first person voice-over on the long-limbed acrobats' exercises, on the dangerous leaps of the macrocephalic dwarfs and the smooth dives of the flying trapezists. Baratier's camera, attached to the trapeze, indulged in the still unusual pleasures of jump-cuts. How could one fail to be charmed? In his outings as a tightrope-walker, 'our little Barat'[2] didn't miss his appointment with the modern cinema and great minds have justly saluted his innovations.[3]

NOTES

1. [The Société des auteurs, compositeurs et éditeurs de musique.]

2. His surname was in fact Baratier de Rey. According to the dictionary, 'baraterie' is old French for 'to dupe, to deceive'. That's why his friend Jacques Audiberti affectionately called him 'the king's smuggler'.

3. Jacques Baratier was born 3 March 1918 in Montpellier. Having obtained a law degree, he was a journalist from 1944 to 1946. Then he became Robert Chanas' assistant on *L'Escadron Blanc* in 1949. His filmography includes: *Les Filles du soleil* (1948, short film), *Désordre* (1949, short film), *La Cité du Midi* (1951, short film), *Métier de danseur* (1953, short film), *Chevalier de Ménilmontant* (1953, short film), *Paris, la nuit* (1956, short film), *Goha* (1958), *Pablo Casals* (1960), *La Poupée* (1962), *Le Comédien et son double* (1963), *Dragées au poivre* (1963), *Èves futures* (1964, short film), *L'Or du duc* (1965), *Le désordre a vingt ans* (1967), *Eden Miseria* (1967, short film), *Piège* (1969), *Goha et après* (1969, short film), *Les Indiens du Brésil* (1969, short film), *La Décharge* (1970), *Vous intéressez-vous à la chose?* (1973), *La Ville bidon* (1974), *L'Araignée de satin* (1984).

AGNÈS VARDA

One evening, I was dining with the witty Catherine Hessling, Jean Renoir's former actress and wife, together with Bill Klein[1] and his wife Janine. Suddenly, Catherine Hessling launched into an enthusiastic evocation of the charms of Porquerolles, a lost paradise. I immediately got the idea of using the cinema to preserve the memory of that island, situated so close to the magic coast I had known as a child.

This was in 1958 and I had just seen a short film by Agnès Varda, produced by Pierre Braunberger, called *Ô saisons, ô châteaux*, a charmingly Ronsardian film with luscious colours, shot by Quinto Albicocco. It had that sense of irritated impatience Agnès Varda used so well: clichés, refined imagery, puns worthy of the Vermot Almanac.[2] I wanted to wed Agnès to Porquerolles. It proved to be the most difficult of all my projects.

Agnès was pregnant. On the day shooting was supposed to start, she would be the mother of a two months old baby. In my judgment, this was not an insurmountable obstacle. Anticipating the possible objection that the film's overly touristic pretext would prompt people to dismiss it as 'déjà vu', I explained to her that this would be something 'never seen before'. *Du côté de la Côte* would outwit the stereotypes of the postcard-documentary ('travelogue' was the word used at the time) with a completely free style.

But there was another difficulty. Agnès didn't know that Coast and it held no magic for her at all. She peremptorily proved this by telling me she had inherited a flat from her father in some mansion near Menton, at Roquebrune-Cap Martin, where Churchill used to stay. She never set foot in it! To try to get her interested, I arranged for her to meet Jacques Prévert over lunch, knowing he would be a passionate defender of the Coast and that she would succumb to his seductive authority. On that occasion, I slipped in another argument, appealing to part of her that identified with the camera as 'superman': 'Only a woman like you,' I insisted, 'can revitalise herself after having a baby by brandishing a camera!'

Agnès still objected that it would be the middle of August and that there would be lots of people about. Our trucks, our technicians and our camera tracks would be submerged by a flood of people. I countered with a proposition that markedly weakened her resistance: 'I will pay top-rent for your flat in Menton and I will pay your sister to look after the baby. That way, every evening you will be able to return to your mothering role in the quiet comfort of your own home.' However, I still hadn't quite grasped the main reason for Agnès's resistance. As an author, she secretly resented the fact that the idea for the project had come from the producer. She had managed to persuade herself that it would be interesting to do a film about the Coast, but that the idea should have come from me struck her as some sort of ontological vice that had to be dealt with by way of a purification ritual. One day, Agnès came and proposed a small arrangement in these terms: 'The film you want me to make is only a commissioned work and you will understand that as an author, I want to make

Agnès Varda

(left to right): *Anne Olivier, Anatole Dauman, Agnès Varda, Michel Mitrani and Quinto Albicocco during the filming of* Du côté de la Côte

a film of my own. I have this idea for a 16mm short, *La Cocotte d'Azur*. I want to catch the guys and dolls of the Coast, the endlessly ridiculous tourists with their weird outfits. It will be a satire on the human condition. You will pay for it and I will make it together with an assistant who will also shoot it. You won't pay me a fee but you will blow it up to 35mm and you will pay me a proportion of the takings.'

Obviously, she was proposing a counter-film, adding a veiled threat should the commissioning producer want to meddle with her authorial intentions. Should he overstep the mark, the producer of *Du côté de la Côte* would be pilloried in *La Cocotte d'Azur* and stand accused in the court of History. Consequently, the wedding of Agnès to Porquerolles had to be clinched by way of a chivalrous joust between the commissioned work and the freely inspired film.

So, while *Du côté de la Côte* was being shot, I simultaneously financed that little *Cocotte*, which unfortunately got me into a row with Agnès that lasted for years. When I viewed the rough-cut, I was appalled by its odious vision of a world teeming with human infirmities, without even a hint of a softeningly comic touch. Trying to be fair to all parties involved, I thought it might be helpful to consult Chris Marker, whom I regarded as the highest authority in matters like this. But Marker's view, heavily influenced by his friendship for his colleague, was extremely positive. Desperate, I called another of Agnès's friends, Alain Resnais, as referee. At the end of the projection, the two directors went into a brief huddle and then Agnès imparted to me a surprising decision. She withdrew her name from the film and left all responsibility for it to the author of the commentary, Paul Guth, to the composer of the music, Joseph Kosma, and to the cameraman who had assisted her. Numerous modifications of the awful rough-cut and the elimination of the most unacceptable scenes resulted in a film lacking any fizz. After a long wait, *La Cocotte* was released as a short accompanying an indifferent Fernandel picture, having suffered the predictable insult of a rejection by the committees grant-aiding quality films.

The commissioned work fared infinitely better. I have pleasant memories of the shooting of *Du côté de la Côte*. In the princely suite we shared in Roquebrune with the crew, I met Agnès every evening at dinner. She was indefatigable and every delivery of rushes confirmed the high quality of her direction. During the editing, which we agreed to entrust to Henri Colpi, even the most moderate remarks I ventured to make about a few places where the pace seemed to drag were received with very bad grace. Henri knew how to use the Montessori method with directors: while they talked he would ever so gently proffer his advice. Except for about thirty seconds, I thought the film was flawless and I doffed my hat to the performance of that great pedagogue.

The commissioned work, generated by crossing one will with another, had a noble career. Thanks to the support of Claude Bruckner, a very fine exhibitor who ran the Vendôme, *Du côté de la Côte* did well accompanying the release of *Hiroshima mon amour*. Because of the success of this unusually, even abnormally long programme lasting over two hours, *Du côté de la Côte* went on sharing *Hiroshima*'s fate in France as well as abroad. At the big festival of Tours, *Du côté de la Côte* came up against very stiff competition, from Alain Resnais himself, from Jacques Rozier and from Jacques Demy, whose life would be changed by meeting Agnès. Film lovers came in droves to this 'fringe Cannes' and *Du côté de la Côte* was warmly received by the public as well as by Jacques Leenhardt's prestigious jury. I later learned thanks to an indiscretion that Jacques Audiberti,[3] who was on that jury, had delivered a scintillating speech paying tribute to 'this completely subjective documentary, this quasi-documentary about the Côte d'Azur'. The jury was about to give first prize to the film when Sylvia Monfort, to the utter amazement of the gathering, solemnly rose up and intoned: 'You all know that I am Madame Varda's actress in *La Pointe courte*. Let me tell you that I am also one of her closest friends. She personally requested me to ask you not to vote for her film which is merely a commissioned work! Otherwise, what would you be able to give Madame Varda for a completely personal work due solely to her complete authorial freedom?' The jury, devastated by this declaration, gave the prize to an animated film by Popescu Gopo.

Would it have given the prize to Madame Varda if it had been accorded the privilege of attending to *La Cocotte d'Azur*?

Twenty years later, at the Deauville festival, I was lying on the beach next to Michel Mitrani. He had been first assistant on *Du côté de la Côte* and remembered the adventure. We were trying to enjoy the benefits of a rather pale sun when we noticed, in a bathing costume and apparently oblivious to the cold, Agnès Varda going towards the sea dragging a towel behind her. I gently called to her: 'Dear lady, thinking of coasts, won't you tell me why you refused the first prize at Tours?' She replied: 'It would have given you too much pleasure, my dear Dauman!'

NOTES

1. The American cineaste and photographer William Klein. Anatole Dauman was to produce his short film, *Broadway by Light*, in 1958. His filmography includes: *Cassius le Grand* (1964), *Qui êtes-vous Polly Maggoo?* (1966, in which A. Dauman can be glimpsed), *Mr Freedom* (1969), *Eldridge Cleaver, Black Panther* (1969), *Festival panafricain de la culture* (1969), *Muhammad Ali the Greatest* (1974), *Le Couple témoin* (1977), *Grands soirs et petits matins* (1968–1978), *The Little Richard Story* (1980).
2. [The Vermot Almanac was launched around the turn of the century, providing the usual agricultural, seasonal etc information. Its recourse to crude humour eventually gave it a reputation comparable to that 'enjoyed' by seaside postcards in Britain.]
3. [French novelist, poet and playwright in the tradition of Mallarmé and Valéry. Best known since World War II for his plays.]

Anatole Dauman during the filming of Du côté de la Côte

CHAVAL AND MARIO RUSPOLI: THE FRIENDSHIP OF PRINCES

CHAVAL

Chaval, the Prince of cartoonists, described himself as a chamber cineaste. His equipment: a 16mm camera he cobbled together, a metronome and his own voice. I met him when Jacques Baratier took me to the modest flat which doubled as his improvised studio.

Chaval was afflicted by a royal melancholia. He wasn't the only humorist to commit suicide.[1] But the distance he had established between himself and the world in no way detracted from his ability to experience deep passions, including one for the cinema.

Les oiseaux sont des cons is a little three-minute film he showed me with his 16mm projector. This short film couldn't possibly be presented to the cinema public in its original format. Nevertheless, it deserved a wide distribution: the word 'con' [literally: cunt. English equivalent: arsehole] occurs about fifty or sixty times in the film. So we transferred it to 35mm, re-recording Chaval's voice, and *Les Oiseaux sont des cons* could be released as a short with the feature *La Permission.*

Chaval left all control over his film work to our mutual friend Mario Ruspoli, who asked me to give it a second life. Chaval's films were admired by his peers in black comedy (Wolinski, Topor, Desclosaux, Siné . . .) and they attracted the wider audiences already seduced by his graphic work. We did the editing and even some shooting. The extraordinary Jacques Dufilho reincarnated the Chavalian universe on the screen in two short films: *Chaval* (1970) and *Le Chavalanthrope* (1972). By means of a 35mm blow-up and a sonorisation that was as faithful as could be to the author, Ruspoli and I also resuscitated a film called *Conte médiocre*, a title with a decidedly Swiftian flavour.

None of Chaval's friends or admirers merited being left out of the gallery of arseholes. None, except one: the strange, funny Mario Ruspoli, his genuine heir, a true Prince, as Chaval used to call him.

NOTE

1. Cartoonist, engraver, writer and cineaste, Chaval, the pseudonym of Yvan Le Louarn, was born in Bordeaux on 10 February 1915. He was a student at that city's Academy of

Fine Arts. In 1929 his father gave him a camera and a Pathé-Baby projector. In 1932 his uncle gave him a 35mm Bell and Howell. In 1936 he became a salesman of pharmaceutical products for the Méladier laboratories in Tours for three years. In 1946 he arrived in Paris and started as an illustrator for *La Gazette des lettres*. From 1948 to 1950, Chaval, still signing his work as Le Louarn, worked for the trade journals of the National Furniture Federation. There he created strips, vignettes and logos. In 1950, ill health caused him to leave Paris for a year and he gave up engraving. He received the Carrizey Prize. In 1953 he received the International Cup for the Best Drawing. In 1956 he got the Émile Cohl Prize for *Les oiseaux sont des cons*. He committed suicide in Paris on 22 January 1968.

RUSPOLI

My old friend Mario Ruspoli,[1] a descendant of a princely Italian family going back to the fourteenth century, is one of the very few Ruspolis who ever worked. According to Chris Marker, Mario's culture was so extensive and his knowledge of languages so brilliant that he could be said to be our Pico de la Mirandola. He died brutally in June 1986, leaving us a posthumous work on the Lascaux Caves which followed on from the four programmes so successfully broadcast on television. The 'Lascaux Corpus' is the first cinematographic monograph about a palaeolithic site. It is a document unique of its kind for the understanding of prehistoric civilisations. Mario's last moments were devoted to re-reading the *Divine Comedy*. I would like to think that, before arriving on the other shore, he glimpsed the luminous presence of a Beatrice.

I can still see the mountain chalet in the middle of the Vaud region, fifty years ago, with its adolescent but cosmopolitan inhabitants reminiscent of the shades wandering through the boarding school described by Valéry Larbaud in *Fermina Marquez*. With my fellow student Mario, we went to classes in Montjoie, exposed more to the heady joys of the snow than to the charms of studying. Already at that time, his inventiveness shone through in the amazing gift of the gab that set him apart from the rest of us. Throughout his life, Mario was to remain deeply immersed in and familiar with the world of myth and he would bewitch his audiences with his storytelling gifts.

One day, in the fifties, I was invited by Colette de Jouvenel to come and see Mario Ruspoli's first film: a documentary about whale hunting as practised by the last harpoonists in the Azores. That's how, in a fairly crowded audience, I met up again with Mario. He embraced me with a beaming smile. At the time, the projection didn't make a real impression on me. I must have been tired because all I remember is that I fell asleep on the strong shoulder of my neighbour, Célia Bertin, who had just written a successful novel, *Une femme heureuse*, which had received the Fémina Prize. So I had to ask to see the film again when towards the end of the evening Mario enquired whether I would agree to make a thirty-minute short for theatrical release out of this film lecture of one and a half hours shot on 16mm. Together with Léonide Azar[2] (the best editor in Henri Colpi's team,[3] I went to see Mario Ruspoli the next day. My mind was preoccupied by an image that had been floating in my memory since the previous night at Colette de Jouvenel's place: the image of a young, blonde woman walking gracefully, preceded by the longest cigarette-holder I had ever seen. This young actress, Isabelle Piat, seemed to be giving the mistress of the house the closest possible assistance. I believe she met an edifying end in some Trappist convent. You can imagine that my mind, beset by this vision of the long cigarette-holder, wasn't very well prepared for a confrontation with the Leviathan and the world of Moby Dick evoked in the credits of *Les Hommes de la baleine*: 'Oyez, good people. The Greenland whale has been deposed. The great Sperm Whale will reign henceforth.' In his work place, by way of a screen, Mario had hung up a large white sheet on which, suddenly, sperm whales started thrashing about. The film bore witness to a happy collaboration between Mario and his sound and image crew, consisting of his companion, Dolorès, and a doctor who was keen on whales. When the projection was over, my friend Azar admitted to having been bowled over: 'I've never seen anything so strong since Eisenstein's images of giving birth.' Unfortunately, I didn't know that part of Eisenstein's work, but I was very impressed nevertheless.

While Mario was abroad shooting for 'Connaissance du Monde', Henri Colpi edited the short film from the lecture-film and Marker wrote the commentary. On his return, Mario found a finished film the inspiration of which didn't seem wholly to coincide with his. True, Colpi and Marker had added somewhat to the original film. But Mario, a princely fellow, eventually declared himself satisfied, the critics having applauded this collaborative effort.

Before producing *Les Hommes de la baleine*, I had to reach agreement with the shipping magnate Aristotle Onassis, who had made the adventure possible with a two million francs loan. When I went to reimburse the potentate, I was most surprised to hear him say: 'Two million plus interest !' I paid him without batting an eyelid and I became Mario's associate, launching *Les Hommes de la baleine* on a tremendous career throughout the world. In Paris, in the Bonaparte cinema, I had collected a glittering audience for the preview which included Chris Marker's *Lettre de Sibérie*. The critics were unanimous in their praise. I particularly remember the eight pages published in *Paris-Match* under the title: 'Corrida of the Sea'.

Encouraged by this triumph and being tired of presenting the 'Connaissance du Monde' TV show anyway, Ruspoli was champing at the bit and kept coming to see 'his oldest living comrade', as he liked to put it. He wanted to get me involved in a new adventure requiring a great deal more resources. In the end, I gave in although the sources for documentaries in the film market had run fairly dry at the time. I managed to secure the collaboration of Michel Brault, the brilliant Canadian cinematographer.[4] I provided him with the prototype of the 'Coutant' camera to enable him to shoot his new project on rural life in Lozère, where he had maternal roots as well as the protection of an obliging 'furuncle', as he affectionately called his uncle from Marvejols, a distinguished progressist parliamentarian. The enterprise eventually led to *Les Inconnus de la terre*, a beautiful title provided by Jean Cayrol to whom we had shown the work-print. Ruspoli went and caught the peasants of the Causse region, some of whom had never seen a cinematographic image. They expressed themselves totally untroubled by the presence of the unobtrusive camera or by the extremely discreet sound recording. The feline and jovial qualities of Ruspoli and of his cameraman enabled them to capture on film the innermost secrets of Lozèrian nature, ordinarily so well guarded and defensive. My friend Michel Zérafa, a writer now deceased, wrote a commentary with a restrained lyricism that suited the subject to perfection. Nevertheless, when it was presented to the Lozérian public, its urban petty-bourgeoisie received the film with some reservations, protesting that 'the Lozère really isn't that primitive: after all, there are bathrooms and there is electricity in the region!'

Not far from Marvejols was the Saint-Alban asylum where Dr Tosquelles had set up the first psychiatric hospital, a pioneering institution, and the methods he introduced there were later adopted, more or less happily, by other institutions. Mario's film, *Regard sur la folie*, paid tribute to the doctors, the nurses and the patients. It is a film animated by the spirit of Dr Tosquelles. As successful as *Regard sur la folie* may be in cinematic terms, it has been perceived primarily as an 'intervention' against the old-style asylum universe. I screened it in the context of my 'Cinéma différent' programme together with *Les Inconnus de la terre*. It stayed on the bill for six weeks at the Pagode cinema, supported by excellent reviews in the press.

The Prince had been enucleated in his youth. His one good eye, in the service of direct cinema, had been directed towards the people he judged to be furthest away from ordinary mortals: whale hunters, the forgotten of this world, those who had been rejected and put into asylums and, finally, cave men. He told me that on me, his pataphysical brother, he had his other eye, the glass one. Alongside the hunters, the peasants and the lunatics, he saw me as part of another condemned species, the artisan of other people's dreams, the silvering on the back of the mirror of the world's images – the 'producer' who always cedes pride of place to the masters of discourse. I believe that the Prince's good eye, that imperishable eye, keeps seeing me as 'directly' as his camera saw those who had disappeared from this world.

NOTES

1. Mario Ruspoli was born in Rome in 1925. After his studies at the Louvre school, he published a number of essays in technical and art journals. He turned to the cinema in 1956 when he made his first documentary feature, *Les Hommes de la baleine*. He went on to make short films: *Campagne romaine* (1958), *Ombre et lumière de Rome* (1959), *Les Inconnus de la terre* (1961). *Regard sur la folie* is a medium-length film made in 1962. He also directed the feature-length film *Petite ville* (1963) and the short *Chaval* (1970). Georges Sadoul described him as 'a master of cinéma vérité, wielding the living camera efficiently, modestly and generously.'
2. Léonide Azar: a French editor of Russian origins. He edited *Paradis perdu* (A. Gance, 1939), *Dédée d'Anvers* (Y. Allégret, 1947), *La Marie du port* (M. Carné, 1949), *Juliette ou la clé des songes* (M. Carné, 1951), *Le Plaisir* (M. Ophuls, 1952), *Ascenseur pour l'échafaud* (L. Malle, 1957), *Les Amants* (L. Malle, 1958), *Austerlitz* (A. Gance, 1960). He also worked with Anatole Litvak, Billy Wilder and Nicholas Ray.
3. Henri Colpi was born in 1921. After his studies at the IDHEC film school, he became a critic (*Le Cinéma et ses hommes*, 1947; *Défense et illustration de la musique dans le film*, 1963). He became an editor in 1950. An all-round man of the cinema, he also co-directed or directed a number of films: *Des rails et des palmiers* (1951, short), *Architecture de lumière* (1953, short), *Une aussi longue absence* (1960), *Codine* (1962), *Mona, l'étoile sans nom* (1965), *Heureux qui comme Ulysse* (1969), *L'Île mystérieuse* (with Bardem, 1973). He is very much in demand as an editor: *La Pointe courte*, *Du côté de la Côte* (A. Varda), *Nuit et brouillard*, *Hiroshima mon amour*, *L'Année dernière à Marienbad* (A. Resnais), *Le Mystère Picasso* (H.G. Clouzot), *A King in New York* (C. Chaplin), *Paris la Belle* (P. Prévert), *La Déroute* (A. Kyrou), *La Joconde* (H. Gruel), *L'Aventure de M. Tête*, *La Femme fleur* (J. Lenica), *Détruire dit-elle* (M. Duras), *L'Hirondelle et la mésange* (Antoine).
4. Michel Brault was born in Montreal in 1928. In 1958 he co-directed a short film with

Gilles Groulx which is regarded as one of the direct cinema manifestos. Fascinated by the development of lightweight cameras and synch sound, he became the leader of the new Canadian film-makers. In 1959 he met Jean Rouch, who wrote: 'All we have done in France in the area of cinéma vérité came from Canada. It is Brault who brought the new shooting technique. We didn't know it and since then we have all copied it.' Cinematographer (in Quebec for Pierre Perrault, amongst others, and in France for Mario Ruspoli, J. Rouch, W. Klein), Brault also directed and produced a significant number of short films and medium-length films.

LES HOMMES DE LA BALEINE

Les Hommes de la baleine, shot more or less at the same time as John Huston's *Moby Dick*, deprives the American film of its last remaining excuses . . .[1] It plunges us so well into the middle of the dangers that we are almost more afraid for ourselves than for the characters. Instead of suspense, which is the rule in fiction films, here we get a feeling of insecurity, sustained by the very instability of the camera and the abrupt veering away of the frame when the beast hurtles towards the frail vessel.

As much as the cameraman's bravery, we must admire the intelligence with which the captured images are constantly put together. It is a lovely idea, for instance, to begin the film with the wrecking of the sloop, so that the viewer straight away gets a clear idea of what's at stake in the struggle, which thus appears to us not just as a sport, a corrida, but as work. Its nobility, as Flaherty taught us, isn't in the least diminished by that.

Our thoughts are expertly but not at all tyrannically guided by Jacopo Berenizi's excellent commentary, free enough to permit itself informative digressions without breaking the rhythm of the images, and yet literary enough to bring to mind the required reference to Melville's great authority, never sinking into pedantry, modest enough to make room for the songs of the island, enthusiastic enough to convey to us the same sense of awe the author must have felt before the events he was filming, making us admire nature and, starting from that, the cinema which is able to sing so beautifully the grandeur of both.

Éric Rohmer
Arts

NOTE

1. [In *Cahiers du Cinéma* no. 67, January 1957, Rohmer had published a long critique of the American film entitled 'Lessons of a Failure: *Moby Dick* by John Huston', reprinted in English in Rohmer's *The Taste for Beauty* (New York: Cambridge University Press, 1989).]

LES INCONNUS DE LA TERRE

Roland Barthes wrote about *Les Inconnus de la terre*: 'It isn't easy to talk about poor peasants. They are too miserable to be romantic, and as they are after all property owners, they don't have the political prestige of the proletariat. It is a mythically disinherited class. On this simultaneously thankless and burning topic, Mario Ruspoli, helped by Michel Brault and Jean Ravel, have managed to make a film that hits the mark, simultaneously enlightening and seductive. His film is a real investigation because he has let these peasants speak, and through their direct, concrete language the overall problems of today's French peasant are immediately represented to us: the meagreness of their income, the backwardness of technology, the opposition of the young towards the old, the conflict between the group and the individual, the demand for a better life linked to that for freedom: before our eyes, a class consciousness awakens and speaks. And yet, in spite of the temptations inherent in the subject, this judicious film is not a sombre film: a flavour, a warmth, a clarity circulate through the images, the objects, the words; there is a reciprocal trust and a living vibration between the camera and these people, these landscapes, between the questioners and the questioned. That's no doubt why here we feel no sense of spectacle and that we look at these images of truth with confidence, pleasure and profit.'

Mme Simone de Beauvoir, for her part, stated: 'Mario Ruspoli has caught the voices of the abandoned countryside. With their very own words, their faces and their silent gestures, he has made the most disinherited peasants in France speak, and suddenly we recognise, in those men forgotten by our age, our neighbours.'

Alain Resnais in Japan
while filming Hiroshima
mon amour

KING RESNAIS

After the Liberation and the end of the war, the film profession ignored the artists who devoted their talents to the making of short films, a marginal sector of the industry supported by the state. An interdepartmental government committee led by the Quai d'Orsay was in charge of the distribution of public moneys. It showed good judgment. Henri Claudel, whom we called The Man's Son[1] out of respect for his father, became our main backer. Innovation encouraged by public patronage found a refuge in the programme accompanying the main feature, before the intermission. In *Le Sel de la terre*, financed under the Monnet Plan, the microphones of Georges Rouquier[2] captured the cry of the pink flamingos and the rustle of their wings. Rouquier, a new Flaherty who managed to catch pure sound in the rice fields of the newly planted Camargue, revealed the power of a cinema at last liberated from the studio.

In that same period, all by himself in his lodgings in the rue des Plantes, Alain Resnais was exploring the work of Van Gogh with his 16mm camera.[3] I discovered that little black and white film using still images at a screening of Les Amis de l'art, an association which met on Saturday mornings at the Lutétia Cinema. It was an informal gathering where painters, historians and critics mixed with cineastes to discuss surprising films. I still remember Pierre Francastel's[4] prolific speeches, the attentive silence of Fernand Léger and especially the gawkish figure of someone I didn't know and who after the screening of *Van Gogh* stood up to give more weight to his words and said: 'I'm telling you, those shots and reverse-angle shots of the Saint-Rémi asylum confirm with absolute certainty that we are in the presence of a great director.' The Amis de l'art constituted a self-selected group where wonderfully talented beginners could reveal themselves as real cineastes without having to go through long initiation periods as assistants. For my first short film with Alain Resnais, I wanted to persuade him to meet the following challenge: to find images for the unimaginable horrors of the extermination camps. I had no doubt that his was the unique talent required for that terrible subject. A number of organisations agreed to finance part of the budget and Poland offered the most significant help: plane tickets, a crew, the lighting of Auschwitz and the camera tracks through the labyrinth along the paths of death. In addition, Argos also made a considerable investment of ten million old francs for a three-reel film. On the advice of Chris Marker, Alain Resnais chose Jean Cayrol, a former inmate of Mauthausen,[5] to write a starkly sober commentary. We took great care to ensure that the German version was absolutely faithful to the original. The poet Paul Celan[6] agreed to

Alain Resnais and Chris Marker

translate his friend Cayrol's text. Our censors had a bone to pick with *Nuit et brouillard*, which Roberto Rossellini judged to be the most important film of the post-war period. They required us to use a trick to hide the cap of a gendarme guarding the victims of the Vel' d'Hiv' raid.

With *Nuit et brouillard*, Alain Resnais acquired a worldwide reputation. And yet, one day in 1957, with a wan smile, he handed me a script written by Bernard Pingaud[7] saying he was ready to shoot it on the spot. Unfortunately, which banker, distributor or competent professional wouldn't reject out of hand a feature film proposal from a certified documentarist? Naturally, the project was turned down. But Resnais soon found a way of breaking into features. Oddly enough, it was by way of a film I had once proposed to Mr Nagata, the president of Daiei,[8] a powerful Japanese film company owning a subsidiary in France called Pathé Overseas. It was to be an officially co-produced documentary about the Hiroshima bomb. The original title summed up the subject in a single word: *Pikadon* (Japanese for the 'flash' of the nuclear explosion). Months went by and Resnais couldn't find any inspiration. When we were beginning to have second thoughts about the whole adventure, he suddenly got the idea to show Japan through the eyes of a woman. A desire for fiction overwhelmed *Pikadon*.

Once the contracts had been signed, the script had to be written. Who to select? Simone de Beauvoir, who was much in fashion at the time, or Françoise

Sagan, who was about to hit the big time thanks to her first novel *Bonjour Tristesse*? As I knew Françoise Sagan, I set up a meeting between her and Resnais in the Pont-Royal bar. She forgot all about it and Resnais had to think again. In the end, he suggested a newcomer to the world of letters and of the cinema, Marguerite Duras.[9] We quickly reached an agreement. She signed the contract and quipped: 'It isn't the golden gate but it's gold all the same: I have my freedom!' Two months later, the script and the dialogues were ready. The hour had struck. Alain Resnais had to leave for Japan on his own, soon to be followed by the scriptgirl, Sylvie Bauderot, and the actress, Emmanuèle Riva. I can still see myself standing by the plane at Orly airport. Firmly shaking my hand as he embarked, Resnais gave voice to his private apprehensions: 'I'm going there to confirm that this film is impossible, simply impossible.' And suddenly, the real danger of the deathleap awaiting this young, reckless producer hit me with full force. Resnais thought it wise to take a picture of me through the porthole of the plane: no doubt he found the expression on my face very entertaining. Was I smiling in disbelief? In Japan, both on location and in the studio, everyone was surprised by Resnais' authority. Without knowing the language he managed to communicate down to the last detail everything he wanted to convey to the Japanese crew and actors. It was a miracle of courtesy! On hearing the good news, Marguerite Duras clapped her hands and swept me along into a salutary sense of elation. Just as well, since my enthusiasm and the takings of my short films augmented by the substantial quality premiums they had received[10] were my only capital. And that, to tell the truth, didn't amount to much in the absence of any distributor's contribution to the budget for *Hiroshima*.

What kind of film had he brought back from Japan? I still didn't know as I didn't want to look at rushes, preferring the emotional experience of viewing the rough cut. One Sunday morning I went to Jean-Pierre Melville's place in the rue de Washington to view a film Jacques Baratier wanted to show me. And what do I see in a room next to the projection booth: a stack of cans containing the rushes of *Hiroshima*, all carefully labelled and sealed with camera-tape. All week long, Henri Colpi and his assistant Jasmine Chasney – whose beautiful legs were greatly admired by fashionable Paris at the time – had been editing the material. Temptingly, Baratier gestured towards a nearby film can: 'Maybe we could look at a few shots?' Surreptitiously, we watched the sequence where Emmanuèle Riva and Okada shower together. Fascinated by this primal scene and overcome with emotion, Baratier whispered: 'A masterpiece, an absolute masterpiece!' Three years earlier, his wife Nena had said exactly the same thing after the first screening of *Nuit et brouillard*. I was struck by that coincidence and, carefully putting the reel back into its can, I sensed that other kinds of shots would be integrated into the film: actuality shots filmed in the flattened city would combine with the perfectly done love scene so admired by Baratier. The documentary would make a forceful return, woven into the very tissue of fiction! I had always been of the opinion that our film should pay tribute to the documentary, which is why, even before the start of the project, I had suggested to Resnais to go and see *Children of Hiroshima (Genbaku no ko)*, a feature film financed by a Japanese teachers' association that had wanted to show the atomic horror through scenes reconstituted in a studio. Its first run lasted only two weeks at the Vendôme cinema, but the amazing force of that 'documentary-fiction' made such an impact on Resnais that he used some of its images in his own film.

After the projection of the first answer print, I slipped Resnais a mischievous note: 'We've seen that already in *Citizen Kane*, a non-chronological film going back in time.' He replied: 'Yes. But with me, it's disorganised.' It is true that *Hiroshima* broke the structure of cinematic narrative and subjected it to the play of affective memory, something François-Régis Bastide described in the following terms: *The past becomes the present indicative all the better to track the future.* Cinema changed. Throughout the world, the public was bowled over by this film, just as with an Edith Piaf song. The text definitely must have contributed to the general emotion. Resnais had meticulously respected the writer's work, even to the point of using a stop-watch to synchronise the tempo of his tracking shots with the moderato cantabile rhythm of the Durassian sentence.[11] However, I think the film's strength basically derives from its *mise en scène* and its skilful editing. At the risk of offending his sense of modesty, I declare that Alain Resnais is well and truly the real author of his films and that, although working with different scripts and with different writers, he addresses us with a unique style which belongs to him and to nobody but him.

One year later, walking along the Champs-Élysées, I happened to bump into Alain Resnais. He told me: 'You can go and see the producer of the film I'm going to make. You will get a piece of it.' As I looked surprised, he added mockingly: 'Your name will do well on the Champs-Élysées.' That's how I came to be one of the six co-producers of *L'Année dernière à Marienbad*[12] with a modest share amounting to 12.5%. Pierre Froment, a man from the old guard, wanted to be the executive producer. I want to spare a friendly thought for this foursquare, honest colleague who opened up Japan to the French post-war cinema when he decided to shoot Yves Ciampi's *Typhon sur Nagasaki* and *Qui êtes-vous M.Sorge* there.

Since critical successes do not necessarily make good money, I still haven't recovered all of my stake in *Marienbad*. But it was a price worth paying for the charming invitation extended to me on the Champs-Élysées by one of the masters of my youth.

Because I had the reputation of being a promoter of intellectual cinema, the film's launch was entrusted to me. The press officer, Constantin Morskoï, whom I had hired for Jean Rouch's *Chronique d'un été*, had a brilliant idea: the Marienbad game, a game with matches inspired by the Go game. All our screenings were held at the L.T.C. laboratory in Saint-Cloud. Batches of augurs and sibyls were invited to go there to consecrate the masterpiece. I myself conducted Sartre there. On this solemn occasion which extracted the verdict 'It's a hundred times better than *Hiroshima*', Alain Robbe-Grillet was delighted to learn that his creative essence had been benevolently looked upon by the great opinion leader. But in spite of the support of the intelligentsia, *L'Année dernière à Marienbad* wasn't selected for the Cannes festival, which has always been

Dedications by Alain Robbe-Grillet and Alain Resnais. The card reads: 'and now I no longer know when – 15 March 1987; For Anatole, whose relentlessness led me to L'Année dernière à Marienbad *(Alain Resnais) and next year where? Oh Anatole!'*

lukewarm towards Resnais. Nevertheless, a few months later, the Venice Mostra awarded it the Golden Lion.

Three years later, Resnais returned to the lagoon and witnessed the triumph of Delphine Seyrig who received the Volpi Cup for best actress for her role as Hélène Aughain in *Muriel*. As the sole producer of this film, I found myself next to them, caressed for a moment by the spotlights.

Muriel was born from my desire to unite Cayrol and Resnais in a new quest for the Grail. My contract with Cayrol for the writing of a script delivered him into the power of one of the world's most intransigent directors. For months we wondered whether Alain Resnais was going to follow up on his project. Day after day, Cayrol provided pages which Alain Resnais would scrutinise severely, saying: 'My dear Cayrol, it's fine up to act III, but act IV continues to cause problems which may well be insurmountable.'[13] And for my benefit he added: 'I'm working on a number of scripts I like. Maybe I'll be forced to abandon *Muriel*?' Those excruciating remarks reminded me of Orly airport and that supposedly impossible film he was going to make in Japan. Cayrol was equally hard on me, appealing for help. His interest in the commissioned script waned visibly, while his desire to make innovative short films with Claude Durand kept growing. Those little 16mm films were ready and awaited only a saviour who at enormous expense would blow them up to 35mm for a theatrical release. I was given to understand that, without such a stimulus, his cinematic inspiration was likely to dry up forever. Perhaps I should think of abandoning *Muriel*? Surprise, surprise: the short films were finally presented to the public and the script of *Muriel* was completed to Resnais' approval. The public liked the film very much. Maurice Couve de Murville, Prime Minister at the time, had been invited to the premiere at the Cinémathèque. Afterwards, he gently told me: 'No doubt the film is a work of genius. But, forgive me, I didn't understand it.' Nevertheless, many books have confirmed *Muriel*'s seminal place in contemporary art. In my view, the film is one of the peaks of Resnais' work, whichever way you look at it: as a way of conjugating cinematic time . . . or as the seduction of a face. Because *Muriel* is also the face of Delphine Seyrig, her forlorn looks, and the 'time of a return', about which more later.

Before *Marienbad*, Alain Resnais' chosen one had enjoyed an uncertain career in the United States, having left France with full confidence in the New World's attractions. In her second bloom as a young actress, she had landed a part in a television series featuring the adventures of a Frenchwoman in the United States. She had a very good contract that accorded her significant raises after every episode throughout the series, but it also tied her down hand and foot. For the duration of her American exile, Delphine Seyrig was thus legally forced to reap the benefits of her television employment. This meant she had to refuse the part of A. in *Marienbad* which Resnais had offered her.

Delphine Seyrig during the filming of Muriel

Ten years earlier, I had been charmed by Delphine disguised as a black cat in Louis Ducreux's fantasy entitled *L'Amour de papier*.[14] Acceding to her wish and no doubt to Resnais' too, I asked a lawyer in Paris to see what could be done. He called the American producer and told him that, on the eve of shooting, his client had decided not to meet her obligations. He granted that breaking the contract would expose Delphine to legal action. But although the court obviously would acknowledge the damage suffered by the American television company, there would first have to be a long and exhausting judicial process in a far away French court. And the damages accorded to the injured party would be damages according to the French system, which is to say, a very modest amount. Finally, if the damages awarded had to be recovered by way of deductions from her salary, it would be from the salaries of an actress who could hardly be considered star material. The American television company graciously accepted this unanswerable reasoning and, pragmatic as ever, immediately found in Annie Fargue a worthy replacement for the part of the Frenchwoman in the United States. By way of that skilfully deployed argumentation Delphine Seyrig was able to play the role of Hélène Aughain in *Muriel*, one of the most interesting parts of her cinema career.

One day when I was telling Alain Resnais, *Muriel*'s demiurge, of my special admiration for the performance of Jean-Pierre Kerien in the role of a sympathetic but unscrupulous con-man, he replied with a contrite smile: 'He looks like me, don't you think?' Decidedly, there is no separating mystification from art.

NOTES

1. [Paul Claudel, Henri's father, was a French diplomat and a mystically inclined Catholic poet and playwright with immense national prestige.]
2. French director born in 1909. He made several short films (*Le Sel de la terre*, 1950) and the famous *Farrebique*, a lyrical evocation of peasant life. *Le Sel de la terre* was released as a short with *Édouard et Caroline* by Jacques Becker. It was Georges Rouquier who spoke the commentary written by Chris Marker for his film *Lettre de Sibérie* in 1958.
3. Re-shot on 35mm with the help of the producer Pierre Braunberger, this short film was to receive an Oscar in the United States.
4. [Leading sociologist and art historian who extended the work of Erwin Panovsky and influenced the re-thinking of film aesthetics in France in the sixties and seventies.]
5. Jean Cayrol was born in Bordeaux in 1911. A poet, he was encouraged by Jules Supervielle, Joseph Delteil and Francis Jammes after the publication of his first collection, *Ce n'est pas la mer*, in 1935. In the Resistance, he was arrested in 1942 and deported to Mauthausen together with his brother who died in Oranienburg. After the Liberation, he became an important novelist (the Renaudot Prize in 1947 for *Je vivrai l'amour des autres*) published by Les Éditions du Seuil. J. Cayrol wrote a book about the cinema, *Le Droit de regard* (Seuil, 1960). In the cinema, he co-directed three short films with Claude Durand: *On vous parle* (1960), *Madame se meurt* (1961), *De tout pour faire un monde* (1962), all produced by A. Dauman. By himself, J. Cayrol directed a short film, *La Déesse*, and a feature, *Le Coup de grâce*, in 1964, starring Michel Piccoli and Danielle Darrieux.
6. Paul Celan (1920–73) was born as Paul Antschel in Chernovtsy (Romania). His parents were deported in 1941 and he was put in a labour camp. In 1947, he left for Vienna where his first book of poems was published, *Der Sand aus den Urnen*. In 1948 he settled in Paris where he has worked since 1959 as lecturer in German at the École normale supérieure

in the rue d'Ulm. He is a friend of René Char, Yves Bonnefoy, André Du Bouchet, Jean Dupin and Henri Michaux. His lyricism can be seen as a means of resistance against oppression. His best known work, *La Rose de personne*, was published in 1963 (by Le Nouveau Commerce). Also: *Enclos du temps* (Éditions Clivages), *Pavot et souvenir* (C. Bourgois), *Poèmes* (Éditions Unes), *Poèmes* (Mercure de France).

7. Essayist, critic and novelist, Bernard Pingaud wanted to find out about the world of film-making. A little later, Anatole Dauman offered him the post of third assistant on Alain Resnais' *Muriel*.

8. Japanese film company founded in 1942 by Masaichi Nagata. Produced films until 1971, when it ceased operating having made films by important directors such as Kurosawa, Mizoguchi, Kinugasa, Ichikawa, Ito.

9. Her novel *Barrage contre le Pacifique* had just been filmed by René Clément.

10. Awarded each year by the Centre national de la cinématographie.

11. At Alain Resnais' request, Marguerite Duras had read her script into a tape-recorder and he had taken the cassette with him to Japan.

12. *L'Année dernière à Marienbad* (1961) was co-produced by Terra Films, Argos Films, Films Tamara, Cinetel, Silver Films and Cineriz (Rome).

13. The film was divided into five acts.

14. This play was performed at the theatre of the Quartier Latin under the direction of Michel de Ré, General Gallieni's grandson.

WE MEANT 'NUIT ET BROUILLARD' TO SOUND AN ALARM

Nuit et brouillard is not only a film of remembrance, it is also a very disquieting film.

We wanted first of all, publicly, to inform or rather 'to draw the public's attention' to the truth about the Nazi concentration camps, one of the images of the racist delirium that in our lifetime grew fiercer than ever.

Of an experience that cannot be comprehended or transmitted, exceeding the bounds of reason, we chose the major images that allowed us, within the limits of a short film, to impart to people alive today a sense of involvement in this huge slaughter, also to those who never tried (or weren't old enough) to understand how far some men can go who hate freedom and who despise their fellow men.

This film isn't some cold reliquary, 'an experience suddenly transfixed', as my brother Pierre wrote, dying in Oranienburg. It is a monument erected in discreet memory of the dead. It is above all a living testimony to the manifestations, so extreme that they beggar belief, of oppression and of force in the service of a system that had no respect for the most basic rights of each and every person in all his singularity and originality.

We have brought into broad daylight the things that, in the archive and in the hearts of the incurable survivors, had become a burden of images proliferating and multiplying to infinity in blood, in cries, in pus. We knew full well that we could only come near the concentrationary reality: a film lasting many hours still wouldn't have been enough to say everything. How to describe those 'Principalities of Murder' where the only possible rebellion was death?

In the indifferent sky of those dry images, one can see the still moving clouds of eternal racism, menacing. They are on the prowl still, threatening to burst in certain places and to knock down whoever remains standing.

A memory survives only in the light cast by the present. If the crematoria are now no more than absurd skeletal ruins, if silence has fallen like a shroud on the grass-eaten ground of the old camps, let us not forget that our own country is not exempt from the scandal of racism.

And that is when *Nuit et brouillard* becomes not just an example to think about, but a warning, an alarm bell for all the nights and the fogs that fall upon an earth which was born in the sun, and for peace.

Jean Cayrol
Lettres françaises, 15 February 1956

Nuit et Brouillard/Night and Fog

Nuit et Brouillard

Argos Films
35, rue Washington
Paris VIII

Paris, 1 July 1958

M. Alain Resnais
70 rue des Plantes
Paris 14

Dear Sir,
  We hereby confirm the agreements concluded regarding the film provisionally entitled
                HIROSHIMA MON AMOUR
which we commission you to direct from the script
written in collaboration with Marguerite Duras who
is also the author of the dialogues and of the
commentary.
  To briefly summarise the film's nature and
subject, let's say that it is a film in black and
white shot in the 1:33 format, lasting approximately
sixty minutes and set mainly in Hiroshima where a
French woman and a Japanese man will have a chance
romantic encounter. The film's experimental character will be underlined by effects involving both
the editing and a soundtrack evoking a 'radiophonic'
and a theatrical tone.
  The present agreement pertains to the following
responsibilities, clauses and conditions which each
of us undertakes to implement and fulfil, to wit:

- the choice of the assistant director, the lighting
cameraman, the camera operator, the editor, his
[female] assistant, the musician and the actors will
be made by mutual agreement. However, your view will
carry special weight in the selection of the
cameraman and the musician.
- it is agreed that the production management will
be discharged by a specially designated person and
that under no circumstances will you be required to
carry out duties incumbent upon the production
manager.
- once the cinematographic adaptation of the script
has been approved, we undertake to respect its form
and substance. Should we for financial reasons not
be able to make the film at that stage, you will be
entitled to retain the payments already received.
- in the light of the favourable character of the
agreement Marguerite Duras has consented to conclude

with us, we undertake to give you every opportunity
to direct the script and the dialogues in full; for
the same reason, we undertake to make a release
print of the authors' version of which you may
acquire one or more copies at laboratory cost.
- in all the publicity done by us or by our
distributors as well as in the credits, we pledge
to mention and to oblige rights-holders to mention
your name in one of the following ways, according
to your choice:

                    a film by
                   directed by

or in any other way agreed by mutual consent. You
can choose the lettering and its disposition in the
credits.
- we will provide you with the necessary equipment
for shooting, which is likely to be a very delicate
process (lighting equipment, a special dolly or
perhaps a small crane, sound equipment, a cameflex,
etc., etc.)

You will be remunerated for your preparatory work
and direction, as well as for ceding your royalties
as specified below, with the total and contractual
sum of 5,000,000 francs (FIVE MILLIONS).

Should a sum of money be allocated to our Company
in respect of the film mentioned herein, as a quality
premium awarded to a short film, a percentage will
be made over to you when our Company has itself
received the eventual amount. The percentages will
be as follows: 10% (ten per cent) of the first four
millions, 15% (fifteen per cent) of the additional
millions.

Should financial aid to short films take another
form than a quality premium, you will receive the
same percentage of the financial assistance that
may be given to the film, according to the law of
6 August 1953 or of any legislation that may replace
it.

The costs you may have to incur for the preparation
of the film will be itemised and submitted to us
every two weeks and we will reimburse them every
1st and 15th of the month. In case of damage to the
camera or of any other incident requiring the
re-shooting of some shots of the film, the additional
days, covered by the insurance, will be paid to you
in addition to your contract.

The rushes and the workprint will not be projected
without your consent.

All your travel expenses necessitated by the film

will be paid by us, as will the costs of your stay outside of Paris.

You alone will be in charge of the artistic and the technical direction of the editing, of the recording of the music and of the mixing up to the delivery of the answer print. The editing rooms and the recording studio where that work is to be carried out will be chosen by mutual agreement between us.

You may, if you think it necessary, proceed with preliminary tests regarding the recording and the mixing studios.

Should you deem the final mix not to be satisfactory, we give you as of now our agreement to consider a new mix.

The editing of the film having been accepted and agreed, the release print will not be modified or cut in any way without your consent.

The making of any eventual cuts will always be entrusted to you.

Answer prints will not be projected without prior consultation with you.

We undertake, should you deem it necessary, to strike the first print immediately after the projection of the answer print.

Should you wish it, we will gladly give you a 35mm or a 16mm copy of the film's release print for your family screenings.

In compliance with all the provisions of this agreement, we become the proprietors, for a minimum period of ten years (or for any longer period should that be agreed by the Society of Film Authors, whose formulas for box-office receipts we agree to from the outset), of all cinematographic royalties and rights necessary to the production and the exhibition of this film and of all the royalties ensuing from your adaptation, your shooting script, your direction and your editing.

This assignment of rights includes the right to realise and to exhibit, throughout the world and by all cinematographic means known or still unknown, in all formats, a talking-sound cinematographic film.

This assignment of rights does not include the right to publish or to represent this same work in any non-cinematographic forms: such as graphic reproductions, printed publications, etc.

However, we shall have the right to disseminate the film by radio or by radiophonic television on condition that the proportion of royalties levied on your behalf by the Society of Authors or by any other organisation remains your property.

You will retain by the same token the royalties owing to you via the Society of Authors, Composers and Music Publishers (SACEM) regarding the film in question.

If for any reason totally beyond either your or our control the production of the film should be interrupted, you will, of course, be able to take on other engagements. The present agreement will not be renewable except by mutual agreement as soon as circumstances permit.

We reserve the right to transfer and assign the present agreement to any third party or company of our choice on condition that we stipulate that you will enjoy equivalent benefits and that we remain joint guarantors with the assignee of the integral implementation of this present agreement.

Should there be a failure to implement any of the stipulations of the present agreement and should a formal notice to that effect have remained ineffective for eight days, this agreement will be legally null and void to the detriment of the defaulting party, the other party being entitled, should it so desire, to full damages.

In the event of litigation concerning the interpretation of the terms and conditions contained in this agreement, jurisdiction will be given to a court of arbitration composed of two arbitrators, one chosen by you and the other one by our company. They will arbitrate, unfettered by any formal procedural rules, and we renounce as of now the right to contest, in whichever way, the verdict they may render.

Should the two arbitrators be unable to agree, they will nominate a third to arrive at a firm decision.

To abide by the formalities, please confirm your receipt of this letter and return to us the enclosed copy duly signed under the phrase 'READ AND APPROVED. AGREED.'

Yours sincerely,

A. Dauman

[signed] Read and approved. Agreed.
Alain Resnais

RESNAIS WORKS LIKE A NOVELIST . . .

Marguerite Duras

We made two kinds of script for *Hiroshima mon amour*. One was the actual shooting script. The other could be called the film's subterranean script.

Before shooting his film, Resnais wanted to know everything: both about the story he would be telling and about the story he wouldn't be telling, concerning the characters we were interested in. He wanted to know everything about them: their youth, their existence before the film and also, in a way, their future after the film. So I made biographies for our characters. And Resnais, starting from these biographies, approached them through images, as if he were relaying through these images a film that already existed about the earlier life of the characters.

When that was done, when the social and the psychological coordinates of the characters had been established, when these characters had been out-lined, through their past and through their future, Resnais demanded that it be clearly established what

Emmanuèle Riva in Hiroshima mon amour

lain Resnais filming Hiroshima mon amour; (below) *Eiji Okada and Emmanuèle Riva*

precisely our interest in them was. Yet another piece of work also related to the film's subterranean script. Usually, directors ask themselves whether the story they want to tell is likely to interest the public. But Resnais asked himself whether the story he wanted to tell would interest him, Resnais. We saw each other every day. And every day Resnais told me what he thought, whether the development of the story suited him or whether it didn't suit him. Not even once have I heard him speak of what would or would not please the future public of his film. Resnais knows exceedingly well what he wants to do, how and why he wants it. Before I knew and worked with him, I could not imagine that a cineaste could be so 'alone'. Resnais works like a novelist.

On top of the social co-ordinates of the characters, of the justification of the story, etc., Resnais asked me to do him a kind of pre-commentary on the images that were to illustrate that story. 'Tell me *how she sees* Nevers in her memory. Tell me *how she sees* the marble coming into the cellar,' Resnais said. So, we invented Nevers as she would see it from the other side of the world. And the entrance of the lost marble in that invented Nevers.

The work I did on that subterranean script of the film is at least as important as what I did on the actual script. What is shown is matched by what isn't shown. Why? Because Resnais wanted, by showing only one aspect of the hundred aspects of any one thing, to be aware of his 'failure' in not being able to show more than one out of a hundred. I believe he always used that drama as a reference point, eminently unavoidable . . . Resnais knew what he wanted; he provoked me and I responded on his terms . . .

Argos Films
4 rue Duphot
Paris I

Paris, 29 September 1962

Madame Delphine SEYRIG
3, rue Maublanc
Paris XV
c/o Paul Olivier
78 Champs-Élysées
Paris VIII

Film: MURIEL

Madame,
   Further to our various conversations, we hereby
confirm that we are employing you and that you agree
to act the part of
                    HELENE
in our film provisionally entitled:
                    MURIEL
directed by M. Alain Resnais.

INCEPTION AND DURATION
   The present contract will become operative between
22 October and 5 November 1962 for a duration of
twelve consecutive weeks.

REMUNERATION
   For the above mentioned period, you will be
accorded by way of remuneration the all-inclusive
and contractually agreed sum of 67,500NF (sixty-
seven thousand five hundred New Francs) which will
be paid to you in the following manner:

3,750NF (three thousand seven hundred and fifty
         New Francs) at the end of each of the twelve
         weeks of shooting, making a total of 45,000
         (forty-five thousand New Francs). . . . .

Photographs taken during the shooting of Muriel, *showing Alain Resnais, Jean Cayrol, Anatole Dauman, J.-P. Kerien and Delphine Seyrig*

SOLITUDES

In our cinematographic world, it matters little to be 'first' or to receive awards at festivals. What matters is to be 'other', and alone, and not to respond to commercial pressures which seem to obey some strange modern programme of depersonalisation.

Isn't it strange that any film which differs from the naive notion of the 'good year for films', as there are 'good years for wine', cannot be made or produced without meeting the kind of obstructions that only used to be put in the way of persistent courage?

The straight line of a beautiful work is as crooked as can be, subject to the twists and turns of each individual's internal labyrinth.

Alain Resnais is privileged to possess such a deep and surging straight line, seeming simple without being so, like that nocturnal family which pretends to behave as if on a leisurely walk.

One would think that his modest submission to the style of his collaborators would separate him from his own problems. Nothing of the kind. The halo of tenderness and respect that surrounds him only shines brighter.

As I can't yet leave my sanctuary, my cineaste friends like to surprise me by sending me their films, of which a long convalescence would otherwise deprive me. In a little rural cinema, I was able to see *Muriel*. It may be that my solitude removed all distraction from my soul and absorbed me into the intrigue so intimately that the work became mine, seemed to emerge from me and to lose the distance of a foreign language.

I was able to attend to the film without the ridiculous 'whys' of Cartesianism. Rare is the race of 'others'. It gathers on a deserted island. *Muriel* is a terrifying masterpiece, swarming with empti-nesses, a microscope on the bacillae of an anonymous world, lost in soulless buildings.

If one had to look for an ancestor of this superb monster, I would cite *Un Chien Andalou*, but here, the drama is worse still, because Alain Resnais heroically shows us a bourgeois paralysis, a hell with no fire.

Jean Cocteau

P.S. I did once succeed in ringing the bell with *Les Parents terribles* and Sartre with *Huis-clos*.

MURIEL

Muriel had to be seen in Venice, because of its yellows, its oranges, its voices as they can sometimes be heard in trains and always in the provinces; the Place Vendôme, Saint Mark's Square.

The voice of a nightmare incessantly evoked by Delphine Seyrig's mannerist style.

The voice of a poetess . . .

How to dissociate Resnais from those voices, because his films seem primarily made of voices, and of ghosts.

. . . The ghost of Emmanuèle Riva like a mute fish in the bowl of Hiroshima; the spectre of Chanel motionless and trembling, hanging from the Marienbad ceiling . . .

That's where the misunderstanding is: in the end, Resnais is the last of the silent film-makers.

Since *Van Gogh*, all led to *Muriel*, the gleam of *Guernica*, of *Nuit et brouillard* and the abstraction of *Styrène*.

For the first time it is no longer an exercise in style and Resnais reveals himself, awakening to his art, and his terrifying modesty has the violence of an octopus: nothing is left of what it crushes.

Muriel marks the arrival of the twelve tone system in the cinema; Resnais is the Schoenberg of this chamber drama.

Like *Hiroshima*, like *Marienbad* and as everyone 'knows and writes', Resnais, who came to the cinema by way of editing, is haunted by time, its dimension, its measure. That's why in *Muriel* he breaks with the uniform subordination to the flow of speech, achieving that sound-counterpoint so often talked about in the old days but never accomplished.

In *Muriel*, the image restored to itself finds its own measure again, the measure of relativity, and in this film where people talk all the time, it lasts and multiplies its duration through the sole power of its intensity.

By disengaging the sound from the image, Resnais freed himself, which is why *Muriel* is his first real film. So ends the journey of a director who seemed to have lost his way wanting to ignore the feature film games, refusing to get away from the constraints of his short films.

This obstinate determination has allowed him to get across the apparently insurmountable wall the cinema had been bumping into for thirty years.

Henri Langlois

BRESSON: DEEP SOLITUDE

We know Robert Bresson's Jansenist motto taken from the Gospel According to John: The wind bloweth where it listeth.[1] One day in May 1965, I had the good fortune to be visited by him. He carried under his arm a script inspired by grace and rejected by all producers. Its title has become famous: *Au hasard Balthazar*. The story of the wanderings of an ass.

I had seen *Pickpocket* in 1959, on 24 December, at the Madeleine cinema, together with some friends I had invited there that evening. All of us were impressed. An almost empty cinema, a masterpiece on the screen: what a metaphor for the state of cinema at that time! Bresson's haughtiness, and his refusal to bend to the rules the professional milieu wanted to impose on him, made him an exemplary being.

After five years of unfruitful approaches to my colleagues, Bresson came to see me on the recommendation of Jeanine Bazin[2] to tell me that *Au hasard Balthazar* would be doomed for evermore unless I gave it some impetus immediately. Shooting would have to start within the six weeks that separated us from the summer. I didn't wish to read the script he wanted to leave with me. It seemed a better idea to listen to the author possessed by his subject. Robert Bresson started by citing a passage from *The Idiot* where Prince Mishkin, visiting the general's wife, recalls a memory: when he was in Switzerland, a stranger to himself and prey to wretched torments, a heartrending cry – the braying of an ass – relieved his suffering. 'An ass. How odd!' the general's wife observed, and her daughters burst out laughing. The laughter that had struck Bresson in *The Idiot* was the same as the one he heard every time he gave his script to a new reader. For five years, his visits to production companies had been greeted with ridicule! In those days, people couldn't imagine getting the money for a film unless there was a star involved. But Bresson's star was an ass. And yet, Bresson's contained passion was so convincing that the project entranced me.

After he told me about the budget he would need for *Au hasard Balthazar* (1,200,000F), informing me that he had received an advance on box-office receipts and had a co-production lined up with Sweden, I took the decision he expected from me: the very next day, preparations for the film would start. But we still had to settle on a contract between us. Bresson suggested I meet his legal adviser. Before we separated, I warned him that I would demand that the author should share financial responsibility if he went over budget. That condition seemed to trouble Bresson deeply. He already saw himself having to confront the unforeseen expenses which he used to heap on some of my predecessors.

The next day, I proposed a very simple clause to his legal adviser: any expenditure over and above the mutually agreed budget would be covered on a fifty-fifty basis by the producer and the author. I was unable to convince my interlocutors of the fairness of my reasoning but I didn't give an inch. As if to clinch the argument, Bresson pretended to leave, and I did the same. We had barely taken a few steps towards the door when the two parties agreed to resume negotiations. We finally concluded an agreement in line with my requirement to split equally any over-budget expenditure.

Two days later, I told Philippe Dussart that I was entrusting the direction of this enterprise to him. This scene took place in front of the Publicis Studio where Agnès Varda's *Le Bonheur* was to be screened accompanied by a short film I had produced.[3] Dussart replied with an indecent laugh: 'Is it really that film with the ass?' – 'Of course,' I replied, looking him straight in the eye . . . A few moments later, sitting in a nearby drugstore, we were identifying the things to be done right away. That's when, having become my accomplice, Dussart revealed to me that Bresson was supposed to go to Mag Bodard the next day to collect his script which, despite warm recommendations from François Truffaut and Jean-Luc Godard, had been indignantly turned down by that producer.

Shooting started near Paris in a natural setting arranged by Pierre Charbonnier.[4] Luckily, the weather was fine and the uneventful first weeks augured well for the future. Such a mood of optimism prevailed in our enterprise that a few days later, Madame Bodard, introduced by Philippe Dussart, suddenly came to ask for a participation in the very film she had so rudely thrown back at the author-director. I knew that when she started out, Mag Bodard had suffered some serious setbacks. *La Gamberge*, a mishap orchestrated by Norbert Carbonneaux,[5] almost sank her. But Philippe Dussart had saved her by giving her *Les Parapluies de Cherbourg*, the Jacques Demy film for which he had masterminded the finance. As for *Balthazar*, the faithful Dussart charmingly pleaded on behalf of the fatally seductive producer: 'My dear Dauman, you will find in Mag Bodard a close friend of Pierre Lazareff, the head of a press empire. With the backing of FRANPAR,[6] your film will be praised to the skies!' In spite of my distrust of joint ventures, I consented to the offer whispered in my ear. It appealed to my shifty and darker side. I betrayed the basic premises of my own enterprise when I momentarily abandoned my conviction that a work should assert itself through its own merits and worth, without the support of some Parisian mafia. I gave in to the temptation of a Faustian pact.

In the meantime, *Balthazar*'s schedule required us to go to the Pyrenees. But it was raining cats and dogs in Ronceveaux where Robert Bresson had located the scene in which action painting was ridiculed during an academic debate overheard by the ass. Alarmed by the weather forecasts, the director decided on emergency action: he had to remain within the budget and that meant finding a dry location to shoot·in somewhere in the Lower Alps. Pierre Charbonnier, who didn't know the region at all, had to go and explore the area at the wheel of his old car. By some incredible piece of luck, within two days he discovered the ideal location not far from Barcelonnette. For the first time,

Robert Bresson

according to Pierre Charbonnier, the most demanding of directors agreed to go and shoot right away in a setting he hadn't personally inspected. The crew's morale remained high until the end of the shoot and the film was finished with everybody feeling cheerful.

I had the feeling it was a masterpiece. Without the slightest anxiety, I invited some friends and acquaintances to the first screening, including Marguerite Duras, Roger Stéphane and Jean-Luc Godard, who proclaimed it to be a masterpiece. Moved to tears, Jean-Luc Godard immediately fell in love with the heroine, Anne Wiazemski, and he married her a few days later. Marguerite Duras was also overcome and she said that all I had to do was ask and she would write a piece of two, three or four pages long. Roger Stéphane gave us an hour on television. All FRANPAR had to do now was to convey the media fanfare to the public. It did so by presenting Mag Bodard as a little fairy princess[7] who had presented the seventh art with a marvellous masterpiece. Today, I no longer feel the bitter taste this mystification left me with for a long time. From *Au hasard Balthazar* I retain the luminous memory of a happy and trouble-free rapport with Robert Bresson. In spite of the little clause regarding the possibility of going over budget, we didn't have a single disagreement from the shooting to the film's release.

Presented at Venice, the film was very well received. François Truffaut,[8] when asked by journalists to give his first impressions of the Mostra, replied: 'They should give the prize for best acting to Bresson's ass!'

Au Hasard Balthazar made a small profit, a miracle due to the combination of the enormous critical sympathy for the film and the scrupulous respect for the budgetary limits. The financial results of *Au hasard Balthazar* can easily stand comparison with Bresson's other films. For instance, the budget for *Une femme douce* was never recovered and Fox, who distributed the film, didn't give it much support. With a budget four times bigger, *Lancelot du Lac*'s commercial fate was appalling: fifty thousand tickets sold in Paris. On the other hand, *Mouchette*, produced by Argos immediately after *Balthazar* but on a smaller budget, rapidly became a classic. It went into profit on its first run and has enjoyed continuous sales ever since.

Hence the stringent necessity for a producer to have a good rapport with his director while keeping both eyes firmly open. It is the best way of serving the author while protecting him from his own demons and ultimate solitude.

NOTES

1. Quoted in the credits of *Un condamné à mort s'est échappé*.
2. [André Bazin's wife.]
3. *L'Invention de la photographie*, directed by Michel Boschet and André Martin in 1964.
4. The great French art director. In addition to *Au hasard Balthazar*, he did the decor for Bresson's *Le Journal d'un curé de campagne* (1950), *Un condamné à mort s'est échappé* (1956), *Pickpocket* (1959), *Le Procès de Jeanne d'Arc* (1962), *Une femme douce* (1969), *Quatre nuits d'un rêveur* (1971) and *Lancelot du Lac* (1974).
5. French film-maker. Directed *Les Corsaires du bois de Boulogne* (1953), *Courte tête* (1956), *Le Temps des œufs durs* (1957), *Candide* (1960), *La Gamberge* (1961), *Toutes folles de lui* (1967), *L'Ingénu* (1971).
6. A media conglomerate belonging to Pierre Lazareff.
7. See Katia Kaupp's article in *Le Nouvel Observateur*.
8. He was presenting *Fahrenheit 451* in competition in Venice.

Anne Wiazemski in Au hasard Balthazar

Robert Bresson directing Anne Wiazemski

SITUATION DU FILM _..MOUCHETTE_____

(définitive)

RUBRIQUE	DÉPENSES RÉGLÉES	ENGAGEMENTS			TOTAL des Règlements et Engagements	SOMMES RESTANT A INVESTI
		3 MOIS		EFFETS		
MANUSCRIT - MUSIQUE						
Droits d'auteurs	2 5.980,-					
Commissions sur droits d'auteurs	3.600,-					
Découpage - Frais de copies	885,65					
Frais de préparation	8.912,09					
Musique	2.500,-					
	2 1.877,74				51.877,74	
ÉQUIPE TECHNIQUE						
Salaires techniciens	2 1.337,58					
Honoraires	3.911,67					
Main d'oeuvre tournage	8.131,09					
Divers						
	3 .380,94				33.380,94	
DISTRIBUTION ARTISTIQUE						
Vedettes au forfait	9.944,49					
Vedettes au cachet	6.155,24					
Petits rôles - silhouettes						
Figuration	1.322,09					
Commissions imprésarios						
	7.421,82				7.421,82	
DÉCORS						
Main d'oeuvre décors	2.601,-					
Indemnités décors naturels	1.750,50					
Meubles et accessoires	100,-					
Frais divers décoration	8.725,77					
Transports décoration	3.655,24					
	6.832,51				6.832,51	
STUDIOS						
Location Plateaux						
Lumière électrique						
Matières premières						
Divers studios						
MATÉRIEL - PRISES de VUES						
Location Matériel	8.627,56					
Frais divers prises de vues	450,-					
	9.077,56				9.077,56	
MATÉRIEL ELÉCTRIQUE						
Groupes Electrogènes	3.983,-					
Location Matériel	0.741,64					
Achat Matériel	1.016,60					
Essence groupes	1.864,36					
Groupmen						
Divers						
	7.605,60				7.605,60	

The budget for Mouchette

PELLICULE et LABORATOIRE

Pellicule négative	46.291,90			6.291,90
Pellicule magnétique	12.545,09			2.545,09
Pellicule positive				
Divers pellicule				
Développement et tirage	42.000,-	1.624,58		3.624,58
Trucages - Générique		8.044,38		8.044,38
Film annonce	1.500,-	695,43		2.195,43
Divers laboratoire		1.691,12		1.691,12
Photographies	3.220,79			3.220,79
	105.557,78			17.613,29

SONORISATION et MONTAGE

Système sonore	5.629,79			5.629,79
Repiquages	5.210,-	377,04		5.587,04
Auditorium	21.363,25			21.363,26
Détection	3.504,-			3.504,-
Salle de montage	2.289,93	5.385,81		7.675,74
Projections	2.511,16	3.276,60		5.787,76
Divers				
	40.508,14			49.547,59

FRAIEMENTS-TRANSPORTS-RÉGIE

Frais de voyage	15.423,72			15.423,72
Frais de séjour	87.286,-			87.286,-
Transports	22.609,11			22.609,11
Régie	27.642,17			27.642,17
Divers				
	152.961,-			152.961,-

DIVERS

Costumes	2.415,57			2.415,57
Maquillage et coiffure				
Publicité	1.936,82			1.936,82
Frais financiers	6.776,59			6.776,59
Registre Public et Enregistrement	1.128,51			1.128,51
Divers	2.500,-			2.500,-
	14.757,49			14.757,49

ASSURANCES

Avant production				
Production	26.916,19			26.916,19
Négatif	11.924,61			11.924,61
Caméras	2.217,52			2.217,52
Mobilier Décor	705,17			705,17
C et Divers	44.283,38	2.519,89		2.519,89

CHARGES SOCIALES et IMPÔTS

				44.283,38
Sécurité Sociale	29.437,09			29.437,09
Congés payés	20.629,40			20.629,40
Impôt sur salaires	17.237,64			17.237,64
A.P.R.I.C.	9.649,86			9.649,86
A.P.R.I.C.A.S.				
A.N.R.A.S.				
Taxe à la Construction				
Taxe d'apprentissage				
Divers				
	86.953,99			86.953,99

TAXE A LA SORTIE	9.990,-			9.990,-
FRAIS GÉNÉRAUX				
PRÉVUS				

THREE RUFFIANS WHO SHOOK THE TEMPLE

Pierre Braunberger[1] and I were born under the same sign. Some people nicknamed us The Dioscuri.[2] If it hadn't been for our age difference, we would have been twins. Our friendship has become unshakeable. On occasion, we found ourselves producing the same directors, such as Rouch, Marker and Godard, the three ruffians.

I was merely a producer, whereas 'Boum-Boum' fancied himself more of an author. He took pride in having quite an influence on the directors employed by his multinational enterprise. I congratulate him for having simplified the job of producing. For him, producing is creating. To hear him talk, Rouch the African was the greatest beneficiary of Braunberger's creative munificence, the Victor Hugo of French production.

NOTES

1. Pierre Braunberger produced (shorts as well as features) fourteen films by Jean Rouch, two by Chris Marker, four by Jean-Luc Godard. Born in 1905, he started as a producer in 1924 with *Catherine* by Jean Renoir. (See also *Pierre Braunberger, Cinémamémoire*, by Jacques Gerber, Éditions du Centre Pompidou, Paris, 1987.)
2. The name given to the twins Castor and Pollux who, in Greek mythology, were the sons of Zeus.

JEAN ROUCH

I admire the film-maker even more than the man. This is not to denigrate the man, an engineer and a tribal poet as well as a faithful friend, but to celebrate the inventive genius of the film-maker of Man.

After the war, he was in Treichville, a miserable suburb of Abidjan, with a second-hand 16mm camera strapped to his back.

Two peasants from Niger, in the process of being proletarianised, offered themselves up to the 'cinema of cruelty' in *Moi, un Noir*: an improvised film

Jean Rouch, Edgar Morin during the filming of Chronique d'un été

made on a non-profit making basis – which would receive the Louis Delluc Prize in 1958 – presenting the African to whom the ethnographer is so close.

The magazine of a Bell & Howell camera holds three minutes of film and that's it. Reloading takes one whole minute: a terrible interruption of spontaneous creativity. Absorbed in playing at cinema, the non-actors forgot to interrupt themselves. In Paris, on the editing table, the richness of the sequence shots stood out. How to edit such discontinuous material? In desperation, Rouch and his editor, Marie-Josèphe Yoyotte, decided to ignore the sacrosanct continuit rules. Another kind of cinema was about to conquer the world.

The tribal poet served the film industry well.

CHRONIQUE D'UN ÉTÉ

The Birth of a Film

Edgar Morin: Jean Rouch and I were at the festival of ethnographic film in Florence in December 1959. I told him it was time he made a film about white people. I suggested a film about love. At that time, a pseudo-scientific film was being prepared on *La Française et l'amour*, and I was dreaming of a film that would itself be a real inquiry into love.

Two months later, we met Rouch and his friends to discuss this project. In the meantime, I had come to the conclusion that it was too difficult to make a real, truthful non-fiction film on such an intimate subject. So I suggested a very simple motif to him: How do you live? This question would be asked of characters from different social backgrounds and would in the end become a question asked of the viewer: How do you cope with life? What do you do with life?

Shooting Methods
Jean Rouch: There were two ways of shooting: with a hidden camera or with the camera in the open. We

used both. We could call it the Coutard-camera method (Raoul Coutard shot *A bout de souffle*) and it consisted of using a long focal lens. Thanks to Coutard's musculature we succeeded in getting images of good technical quality without using a tripod and while shooting from a great distance. People didn't know they were being filmed. It is a kind of image hunt. So, Coutard did the Renault sequences for us. The other method is to use very short focal lenses, so that you are very close to the people you are filming and pretty soon the presence of the camera ceases to be important to them. We played the game with people who were amenable to this way of working. We told them: 'We are filming. If you want to censor something, say so.' You have to be honest!

Actors and characters
Edgar Morin: Everyone expresses himself by adopting a mask that very much resembles his own character. It is a bit like asking an actor to embody himself and to react. It is a psychodrama. No script has been prepared. We put people together and what will happen gradually begins to take shape.

Influences
Edgar Morin: Our enterprise is related to all the neo-realist and neo-documentary currents (such as the British Free Cinema, Rogosin's films[1]) and continues along the lines of Rouch's previous experiments. But although it is close to documentary in that it contains no element of fiction whatsoever, it is something different because it tries to go to the heart of people's personal problems. Let's say: it is 'cinéma-vérité', looking for both objective and subjective truth.

Extracts from *France-Observateur*,
22 December 1980
and from *France-Forum*, March 1961.

NOTE

1. [A North American documentarist born in 1924; best known for *On the Bowery* (1955) and *Come Back Africa* (1959).]

Filming Chronique d'un été

CHRIS MARKER

Chris Marker brings a new meaning to the relation between sound and image. In his work, the word irradiates the image and achieves its true cinematographic status. To evoke the life of this secretive man is to risk his anger. There are plenty of legends about him and it isn't up to me either to confirm or to demolish them. I won't go in for gossip. The only thing that counts is the work. One could speculate forever about the female actress in *La Jetée* but to what purpose? Is *Alice in Wonderland* just the luminous trace of a charming moment between Charles L. Dodgson alias Lewis Carroll and the little Alice Liddell one day in July by the river bank?

Chris Marker is an unknown man. He avoids the press, the radio, television, refusing his image to any of them. Only one time did I see him break his own rule. That was at the Venice festival where, after the screening of *Le Joli Mai*, he faced the press. No doubt motivated by lofty revolutionary principles, he had come physically to defend his film.

Henri Michaux,[1] who had a high regard for him, paid tribute to his erudition in this way: 'We should flatten the Sorbonne and put Chris Marker in its place!' As some people saw analogies between *Plume*[2] and Marker's style, I wanted to get things clear. When at some exhibition of modern art I noticed the shaven head of our friend Marker, I leant over towards the bald pate of Michaux and asked him about these alleged affinities. 'Analogies?' he whispered, 'Not in politics, at any rate.'

One of the first meetings of the committee grant-aiding quality films saw *Lettre de Sibérie*, and one of the Honourable Men, chosen from among the most brilliant people of the time, wondered about the source of the commentary. Michaux perhaps? The letter began: 'I am writing to you from a distant land.'[3]

Every day on my way to the office I pass by the Lycée Pasteur, but that isn't where I got to know Marker. He was a few years ahead of me. I owe that meeting to Alain Resnais, who had organised a screening of a 16mm film, still being edited, by one of his friends.[4] That film was to become *Dimanche à Pékin*, shot in colour on 16mm. Hidden behind his film, Marker seemed loath to talk, leaving it up to Resnais to talk to me instead. 'What you have just seen is very good; only the sound is still missing. Paul Paviot financed the shoot. You should get together with him to produce a soundtrack.' I very gladly co-produced this modest little film, modest as far as the finances were concerned but strikingly innovative. Shown at the Tours Festival (the Cannes of short films) this poetic essay about China received the first prize. Today, it could be seen as the last of the 'hundred flowers'. In fact, *Dimanche à Pékin* wasn't Marker's first film: that was a film about the Helsinki Olympics, seen by only two or three privileged friends.[5]

In spite of all his secrets, everybody knows that Chris Marker set up the Petite Planète series for Le Seuil, that he is one of the great photographers of our time and that he is the author of the youth novel *Le Cœur net*, although he undeservedly omitted this book from his biography. His actual civil status isn't as mysterious as it is made out to be since it was recorded in the register of Neuilly's Town Hall. I have in my possession some photographs, faded to yellow, with exotic people displaying a family, supposedly his, the Krasnapolskis. But legends transform themselves into reality and in the end you wind up being what you have become: a stranger.

At the time of the Khruschev thaw, the France–USSR Association and the cultural department of the Soviet Foreign Office agreed to sponsor a new kind of film operation. They would open up Siberia, that pioneering land, and make it available for the curiosity of a Western film-maker known to be in sympathy with the Communist ideal, loyal yet hostile to the socialist realist aesthetic. The charm offensive seduced our globetrotter and he in turn recruited me, guaranteeing that the project would be conducted with absolute freedom and that this would extend to the crew's need to move about as well as to the director's fantasy. On the Soviet side, considerable resources had been put at our disposal: planes, ships, resting places, reindeer herds, Yakut opera, guides and interpreters. *Lettre de Sibérie* benefited a great deal from that hospitality. That is how Sacha Vierny, Armand Gatti and André Pierrard, our mahout, came to plant the Argos flag not far from the polar circle.

When he got back, Marker announced, no doubt to scare me: 'I don't know whether we'll ever get a film out of all this. Well, we'll find out soon enough, after a few months editing.' The great cineastes have a habit of putting the frighteners on a Maecenas with remarks like that. I reassured him that he would be able to edit his film as he wished, that he could take the time he needed and that I wouldn't put any pressure on him. For the release, I added the short made by his friend Ruspoli, *Les Hommes de la baleine*, for which Marker had written the text using another pseudonym.

Before the premiere, I wanted to thank our Soviet friends and I invited the Embassy staff to a cocktail party at the Publicis on the Champs-Élysées. The ambassador, Vinogradov, was the guest of honour. No sooner had 'The End' appeared on the screen than the ambassador, ignoring the lavish buffet, rushed towards the exit with two dozen advisers in his wake. I tried to detain them, calling out to the most Parisian of the diplomats: 'Would you mind at least telling me what you think of the film you have just been shown?' The answer fell like the guillotine's blade: 'Let me inform you, dear Sir, that there is no such poverty in Siberia!' Embarrassed, the vice-president of the France–USSR Association, 'comrade' Pierrard, stuttered: 'His Excellency has his rules.' Chris had already experienced some mishaps with the lords of the manor. The Chinese had some very harsh words for the man who had dared to show a woman with bound feet, a humiliating reminder of the old days, in a shot in *Dimanche à Pékin*. North Korea had been just as hard on him, when two thousand dignitaries, at the screening of the short film he had just shown them, received it in icy silence.

Not in the least discouraged, Marker's ideological wanderings later extended to Cuba, cajoling the 'fraternal friend' for a while.

Next year or the year after that, I will start with our friend Marker on his magnum opus, a science fiction film located in Okinawa. The war sequences

Chris Marker (left) *and Armand Gatti during the filming of* Lettre de Sibérie

will provide an opportunity to put the computer's image-treating capacities through its paces. Fiction and documentary will intermingle, endowing the nature of things with an air of uncertainty. Tragedy and humour will make common cause. The great 'artifex' has the floor.

Contrary to the Politburo, Marker's political wanderings have never upset me. For thirty years I have remained faithful to this protean genius, to this intelligence that rises above genius.

NOTES

1. [Francophone Belgian poet and painter, best known for his long narrative poems recounting imaginary voyages and fantasies; author of *Un Certain Plume* (1930) and *Ailleurs* (1948).]

2. [Mr Plume was a first-person character invented by Michaux.]

3. Chris Marker's tribute to Henri Michaux's *Lointain intérieur*.

4. The screening took place in a minute viewing room called Red Star, on the sixth floor of the rue Lamennais.

5. Chris Marker's filmography: *Olympia 52* (1952), *Les statues meurent aussi*, co-directed with Alain Resnais (1953), *Dimanche à Pékin* (1956), *Le Mystère de l'atelier 15*, co-directed with Alain Resnais (1957), *Lettre de Sibérie* (1958), *Les Astronautes*, co-directed with Walerian Borowczyk (1959), *Description d'un combat* (1961), *Cuba si!* (1961), *La Jetée* (1962), *Le Joli Mai* (1963), *Le Mystère Koumiko* (1965), *Si j'avais quatre dromadaires* (1966), *La Sixième Face du Pentagone*, co-directed with François Reichenbach (1968), *A bientôt j'espère* (1969), *Le Deuxième Procès d'Arthur London* (1969), *Carlos Marighela* (1970), *La Bataille des dix millions* (1971), *Les mots ont un sens* (1971), *Le Train en marche* (1973), *La Grève des travailleurs de Lip* (1974), *La Solitude du chanteur de fond* (1974), *L'Ambassade* (1975), *Le fond de l'air est rouge* (1977), *Sans soleil* (1982), *A.K.* (1985).

RENAISSANCE OF THE SHORT FILM

Chris Marker's *Dimanche à Pékin*: Grand Prix of the Short Film, 1956

By François Truffaut (*Arts*, 21-27 November, 1956)

Thirty-four shorts of which thirteen were 'in competition', fifteen hours of screenings in three days, that's the tally of the Second International Festival of the Short Film in Tours. The jury, presided over by Georges Auric and consisting of Mme Nicole Vedrès and Messrs Jean de Baroncelli, Emmanuel Berl, Jean Effel, Goerg, Roger Leenhardt, Man Ray, M. Gallichon and J. Verdier have awarded the Grand Prix of the Short Film, 1956 to Chris Marker's *Dimanche à Pékin*.

Chris Marker is the author of a novel, *Le Coeur net*, and of an essay on Giraudoux. He came to the cinema collaborating on a number of Alain Resnais' films and together they made, on the negro arts, *Les Statues meurent aussi*, which still awaits its censorship certificate.

Dimanche à Pékin, which Chris Marker was able to make thanks to Paul Paviot, is a sort of diary of his recent journey to China. Shot in 16mm and blown up to the commercial 35mm format, the value of this exotic film resides in the 'tone' of its narration, the beauty of its commentary and the firm editing more than in the quality of its images. What the jury gave the award to, I assume, is above all the perfect way in which the haphazard and necessarily limited material has been 'highlighted'.

A special mention distinguished the plastic qualities of François Reichenbach's essay, *Impressions de New York*, which won over the Tours public with its astounding photographic bravura.

Goods, Memory and the Dawn

Les biens de ce monde by Edouard Molinaro is an adroit and ingenious documentary about 'the bank'. The 'symbol' of money becomes a pretext for an irreverent report on the banking world where vaults evoke prisons: Sing Sing as a long-term lender.

In Alain Resnais' remarkable film about the National Library, *Toute la mémoire du monde*, every image also implicitly refers us to that concentrationary universe. Those piles of books, labelled, numbered, identified, vaccinated, looked after, microfilmed, all those stacks and boxes come straight from some other Xanadu, a Buchenwald of the mind. It is an admirable film confirming Resnais' position at the top.

René Lucot's excellent film on the atom, *A l'aube d'un monde*, has a commentary by Jean Cocteau. There is controversy around this much-attacked commentary, but in my view it is splendid. Since poetry is the art of the best and the most precise word, I don't see who else but Jean Cocteau could have conducted us through this extraordinary world. Amongst Jean Cocteau's recent texts, that for *A l'aube d'un monde* is the most brilliant.

The Shepherd and the Clog-Maker

It is difficult writing about the film of a friend, especially when it is a good film and one's best friend. I have followed the making of Jacques Rivette's first featurette, *Le Coup du Berger*, too closely to be able to take sufficient critical distance. Like almost everyone else, I particularly love the ironic and unusual tone of this story based on an actual event, admirably directed and very well acted by Virginie Vitry, Anne Doat, Jean-Claude Brialy and Etienne Loinod, a pseudonym sheltering, as all lovers of anagrams will recognise, one of my most distinguished colleagues.[1]

Le Sabotier du Val de Loire, which could be aesthetically located between Robert Bresson and Georges Rouquier, reveals a talent that holds promise for the French cinema: Jacques Demy. With intelligence, taste and tenderness he paints a detailed picture of a clog-maker. This first film, by the very nature of its ambitions, was very difficult to bring off successfully. With hardly a false note, Demy has managed to do it.

The Bottom of the Bin

If the selectors had been a little more demanding and also a little less diplomatic, it would have been possible to eliminate from the competition four or five films that had no business being there. The only thing to be said for *De Pantin à Saint-Cloud* is that its author, Pierre Gout, is very nice. *Le Voyageur* massacres a poem by Guillaume Apollinaire by way of about thirty incredibly ugly drawings. (Henri Gruel, the sympathetic director of animation films, is responsible only for what's best in the film: the animation of the drawings.)

The tedious *Au Paradis des Images* by Philippe Agostini arbitrarily hits us over the head with one Epinal image after another, while Marc Maurette didn't exactly bust a gut either to film three or four *Danses de Chine*. But the worst film shown in Tours was the one by Louis Weiss: *La Sainte Colline de la Victoire Morale*, unworthy of even the rankest amateur.

La Symphonie pour un homme seul, a lousy, misogynist ballet crudely filmed by Louis Cuny, shows up the negative aspect of the 'quality premium' [subsidy]: it incites a mediocre film-maker to bluff himself as well as bluffing others.

However, in spite of these regrettable 'exceptions', this year's selection was infinitely superior to last year's thanks to the encouragement provided by that premium and the confidence it creates in the profession.

The French short film is awakening at last.

NOTE

1. [The reference is to Jacques Doniol-Valcroze, critic and co-founder of the journal *Cahiers du Cinéma*, to which both Truffaut and Rivette contributed, and later himself a film-maker.]

Argos Films
35 rue Washington
Paris VIII

Paris, 29 July 1957

M. Chris Marker
c/o Editions du Seuil
27 rue Jacob
PARIS (6ième)

Dear Sir,

Further to our various conversations, we hereby hire you as director for the provisionally entitled film

BAIKAL

Summary

The film will be shot in Eastern Siberia throughout September and October 1957.

The theme of the essay, which you will make in colour, will be one of the least-known areas of the Soviet Union bordering Mongolia. The exploration of that region, the study of its human and economic geography, will help define the subject you are proposing to film.

1. *Rights*

You cede to us all adaptation and television rights, in all languages and in all forms, in all known and unknown formats; the rights to the scenario, the shooting script and the commentary of which you will be the sole author.

2. *Direction and Editing*

In exchange for ceding all the above mentioned rights, and for your overall collaboration thus defined, including the direction of the editing, you will receive the total and contractual sum of:
- one million Francs if the final cut of the work copy in 35mm should be less than 1,300 metres;
- 3,250,000 Francs should it be a feature film.

The dates of payment will be agreed by mutual consent. However, a first payment of 350,000 Francs will be made to you on completion of shooting and the last payment will be made on delivery of the release print.

Please be so kind as to confirm your agreement to the above by returning to us the enclosed copy duly signed preceded by the statement 'Read and approved. Agreed'.

Yours sincerely,

A. Dauman

Extract from an interview with Chris Marker by Jean-Louis Pays in May 1962 for the journal *Miroir du cinéma*

Jean-Louis Pays: Tell us something about your projects. You want to make a feature film?
Chris Marker: No, that's neither here nor there. If this should be suggested to me, it will depend on the circumstances, but I have 'absolutely' no 'wish' to make a feature film. Besides, the length isn't what counts.

Q. Would you like to direct actors?
A. Not at all. I am an essayist, not a novelist. You speak of a revolutionary cinema as if there were a revolutionary printing press. Cinema is a system that allows Godard to be a novelist, Gatti to do theatre and me essays. That's all. There is no connection between those films.

Q. Except for Israel, up to now you have been in countries that have had their revolution. There aren't many left.
A. What's left are the ones who will have theirs. My dream is to receive an annual salary for wandering around the world with a camera. Then I'd be really happy. Maybe I'll make a feature one day, I don't know. So many bizarre things happen in life.

Q. What did you do on *Nuit et brouillard*?
A. Nothing at all. I was there . . . When things get difficult, Resnais quite likes having someone around who will tell him what he's already thinking so that he'll be able to say there was someone else. I played that role.

Q. He's a good friend?
A. I think so!

Q. Resnais said that *Marienbad* was a mirror; but some people think it leads nowhere and that Resnais is in a dead end.
A. Someone who goes down into the metro without knowing it may think that's a dead end too. I don't agree at all. After *Marienbad*, many films become impossible – I don't know which ones – and others become possible. At any rate not those which try to remake *Marienbad*. After all, whether it opens things up or closes them down, who cares? Whether a

masterpiece opens doors or closes them is irrele-
vant. That's not the author's problem. It's a problem
for others. It's enough that a film . . . well,
nobody went further in that particular direction
and that alone is a value in itself. That's
commitment.

Q. Do you think he is the greatest French director?
A. Without a doubt.

Q. The greatest in the world?
A. I wouldn't say that because there are so many
different kinds of directors, but if there are ten
people who have changed something in the cinema,
he's one of them – if there's only one, it may well
be him.

Q. You must find it funny when the critics say
'Godard is a fantastic guy'.
A. Godard has contributed a lot . . . Not just
formally, but to the spirit of cinema as well.
A bout de souffle is an extremely important film in
the history of cinema. I don't know whether it will
retain its value as a specific piece of work. There
are lots of works like that in literature which were

Chris Marker

absolutely indispensable and one is grateful that
they exist but later nobody reads them anymore. I
don't know whether in fifty years time people will
still go to see *A bout de souffle*. They may well do
so. It was very important.

Q. That woman who betrays the man she loves, doesn't
that seem bizarre?
A. That's the subject, it's a character. As for me
. . . I have the impression there is an ellipse at
the end of the film. What happened between the two
of them that night? We don't know. Were they going
to hang on to that? We didn't find out. But the
reasons for the betrayal are complex. At any rate,
it's a Stendhalian film . . . . Godard's mistake
. . . is that the Fabrices of another era aren't
quite up to the aesthetic level of the ones in our
time.

   And if you were to take the character of Fabrice
just in social terms, he's a nasty little git. But
he is the particular embodiment of the value of
youth, which Belmondo takes on and incarnates. And
that's now caricatured as 'Belmondism' and 'Godard-
ism'. But in so far as this figure appears to embody
something that's able to shock the sectarians, there
is something very healthy about him. A kind of
anarchic spirit . . . . There is a sense of brute
energy about him which could just as well take the
exact opposite form.

   Godard's charm, even though I profoundly disagree
with him on important points, really is that he says
anything. So chances are there will be some very
good things, things that wouldn't get said except
by people who are prepared to say anything, because
there is a kind of spiritual anarchism that cannot
stand being channelled. People aren't mad in a
right-wing or in a left-wing sense. When you are
mad, you are mad both on the right and on the left.
And then it takes a certain form and that's the
spirit of *Le Petit Soldat* - I haven't seen it, which
is a pity because you have to defend it on principle
since it was banned. You must defend banned films
even if you don't like them.

Q. Is it Resnais who made you want to make films or
did you want to make them already?
A. I have always wanted to make films.

Q. You are thirty-nine years old now?

A. Forty, my boy.

Q. So you have known Resnais for twelve years?
A. More than that. Just after the war when I was working for Labour and Culture[1] and he was wearing a cassock playing a priest in a piece by Pirandello. One remembers things like that.

Q. Was your first contact with the cinema *Les statues meurent aussi*?
A. The first serious one, yes.

Q. And before? Did you write scripts, try things?
A. No. Well, little bits on 8mm that were rather awful.

Q. Oh! You made 8mm films. Can we see them?
A. No. Absolutely not. No way!

Q. Do you know Resnais' 16mm films?
A. Oh that. Resnais' 16mm is something totally different. I don't want to talk about them because Resnais would be furious . . . . He made things on 16mm which one day should be the concern of cinémathèques.

NOTE

1. ['Travail et Culture' was an organisation close to the French Communist Party, set up after the Liberation to stimulate cultural life. André Bazin directed its film section.]

Alain Resnais

SUNLESS

An unknown woman reads and comments upon the letters she receives from a friend – a freelance cameraman who travels around the world and is particularly attached to those 'two extreme poles of survival', Japan and Africa (represented here by two of its poorest and most forgotten countries, even though they played a historical role: Guinea Bissau and the Cape Verde Islands). The cameraman wonders – as cameramen do, at least those you see in the movies – about the meaning of this representation of the world of which he is constantly the instrument, and about the role of the memory he helps create. A Japanese pal of his, who clearly has some bats in the belfry (Japanese bats, in the form of electrons), gives his answer by attacking the images of memory, by breaking them up on the synthesiser. A film-maker grabs hold of this situation and makes a film of it, but rather than present the characters and show their relationships, real or supposed, he prefers to put forward the elements of the dossier in the fashion of a musical composition with recurrent themes, counterpoints and mirror-like fugues: the letters, the comments, the images gathered, the images created, together with some images borrowed. In this way, out of these juxtaposed memories is born a fictional memory and in the same way you sometimes see a message in a hall saying 'The porter is upstairs', we would like to preface this film with a placard: 'Fiction is out' – somewhere.

Chris Marker

JEAN-LUC GODARD

Cannes 1964, at the end of the convivial festivities. The Carlton was returning to normal, the posters had been swept away, the stands in the hall were being dismantled and the long corridors were deserted. I noticed Godard, who had come for the last twenty-four hours. He told me that he would be going to Porquerolles the next day to shoot his new film, *Pierrot le Fou*, starting with the final shots. For the sequence preceding The End, where Belmondo has his head wrapped in dynamite and is about to blow himself up, Godard had chosen the Argent beach.

Suddenly, in a flash, I remembered the young Godard coming towards me during the Tours Festival. He had just seen Agnès Varda's *Du côté de la Côte*, the last shots of which show the Argent beach, images of a lost paradise. I can still hear him telling me with a voice touched by emotion: 'What a great film!'

Six years had passed since *Du côté de la Côte*. Abandoning the dream of total and perfect joy imagined by Agnès Varda, Godard was going to Porquerolles to try and find, under the sign of the beach,[1] the joys of loss. *Pierrot le Fou* was Godard's most popular film and the least popular Belmondo picture. Previously, the market in Godard stock had been very depressed. He had given the cinema, one after the other, *Les Carabiniers* (1963) and *Bande à part* (1964). Both films registered record non-attendances in spite of the deserved praise from writers, poets and critics.

Nevertheless, in 1964, Jean-Luc Godard started making *La Femme mariée*, a film long banned by the censor but which, once released, would soon buoy up the value of the Godard stock. The troubles with the censorship office, presided over by a certain Mr de Segogne, concerned a minimum of twenty cuts and there were even serious problems with the title itself. A married woman who commits adultery: unthinkable! Georges Pompidou, who was Prime Minister at the time, became involved prompted by Pierre Lazareff who sought to quieten things down. Many voices loudly demanded freedom of expression in France. Georges Pompidou leant on the censors and a certificate was granted on condition that the film would not be called *La Femme mariée*, suggesting married women routinely committed adultery and that this was quite normal, but *Une femme mariée*, suggesting that this was only one particular woman, a black sheep, a historical accident. Reviled by the censors and shunned by the market, Godard became an international star. Whenever we met, I was always taken aback by his glum look and the brown shoes that went with his black suits. Adding to his paradoxical dandyism, he usually wore a tatty, ill-fitting raincoat. Such lapses in good taste would have struck an English person as major offences. But the miscreant was, at heart, friendly and charming: a good companion rather than a Marxist comrade.

It wasn't easy to mount a film with Godard but I nevertheless wanted to court the diva's talent in my way. The public hadn't appreciated that in my diptych of *Crimes of Love*, Alexandre Astruc's *Le Rideau Cramoisi* had been coupled with Maurice Clavel's *Mina de Vanghel*. I liked *Mina de Vanghel*, 'a hefty

Jean-Luc Godard with Marina Vlady during the filming of Deux ou trois choses que je sais d'elle

mouthful of poison' admired by André Breton and Benjamin Péret. But I dared hope that the elective affinities of Godard and Astruc might engender a new *Crime of Love* worthy of replacing *Mina*. Godard accepted the idea and he proposed an adaptation of a story by Maupassant, *Le Signe*. The plot is well known. It concerns a middle-class woman who, through her window, spies on the doings of a prostitute. Through some unconscious act of mimicry she impulsively addresses a smile to a passer-by and finds herself drawn into a strange confrontation with this unknown person who misunderstands her intentions. Will she be able to escape the extreme consequences of the fantasy that is taking hold of her?

I was seduced by the cinematographic libertinism to which Godard wanted to turn his talent. Two or three days before the start of the film (initially called *Avec le sourire*), Godard showed me a photograph from *France-Soir* showing an Italian actress answering to the radiant name of Mari-Lu Tolo. She had arrived in Paris to conquer the world of cinema. I was enthusiastic. The day before he was to start shooting, Godard bluntly announced that he was in no condition to direct because of his blood pressure. I got worried: 'What is your blood pressure?' He replied: '12 over 8', which is, as everyone knows, excellent, to say the least. Aghast, I looked at the production manager, Philippe Dussart, Godard's associate. Livid, Dussart insisted that the first contractual payment would be reimbursed to me. 'Not at all, my dear friend,' I told him, 'let him keep the money for a future occasion. His blood pressure will be all the better for it.' I was secretly hoping that soon his inspiration would flow again, restoring his blood pressure to normal.

Sure enough, soon after that Godard came to see me with a disarming smile to announce that he was going to direct Jean-Pierre Léaud in some further adventures of Antoine Doinel in between the episodes of Truffaut's series. That's how *Masculin-féminin* came about and the film was to bring me some delightful moments. On the first day of shooting, Godard appeared briefly in front of the assembled crew and mumbled, barely intelligible: 'I'm not in form today.' Then he left. The next day, all ears were again straining to capture some whispered sentence and again, the same story. While the crew withdrew in silence, I felt cold drops of sweat running down my temples. The third day was the right one: the film got off to a start with five usable minutes. It was finished in three and a half weeks. Godard and I shared the production fifty-fifty. *Masculin-féminin* proved to be a worldwide success and it made us a happy pair of co-producers.

Both of us wanting to follow up such a fine association, we decided to make another film in Techniscope entitled *Deux ou trois choses que je sais d'elle* (1967). This splendid film was set against the background of the huge new housing developments in the Parisian suburbs. Godard would transform the architectural misery of the place through the extreme beauty of his images. The overall atmosphere was very propitious for his work. The release of *Une femme mariée*, tried and crowned as it were by the censor, brought him enormous success, flavouring admiration with a touch of scandal. Two weeks into the shoot, Godard was struck by a bright idea that sounded more like a catastrophe to me: 'Beauregard is in deep trouble. I shall make a film to help him out. I'll do it quickly and right away and it will be called *Made in USA*.' So it happened that he made both films at the same time, resulting in a dangerously simultaneous release. His justification was that 'Painters are able to exhibit in different galleries at the same time, so why not film-makers? Spectators will be able to go from one queue straight to the other. Their interest will be all the keener for it!' In his subtly masochistic smile I could read the ruination he had thus inflicted on both films, destined to destroy each other by halving the number of viewers for each of them. I was mortified. Thinking about it more calmly, in the discomfort of that double-headed release, I understood that with *Deux ou trois choses* Godard had wanted to simplify the representation of that phantasm of prostitution which at one time he had approached with such accuracy in his adaptation of Maupassant's *Le Signe*. In prostitution, the whole mechanism of which he had laid bare already in *Vivre sa vie*, Godard saw nothing but the objective effects of a male oppressive system. I disagreed. My view is that prostitution is not a domain reserved for certain women but the most enduring and the most widely shared phantasm in the world. For instance, if you consider the things a settled, respected man, eager for public recognition, can yield to – how he dresses himself up and sheds misleading disguises, how in his life furtive deceptions and public statements are interwoven – you can see how Godard's notions are, in spite of himself, rather sociological, manichean and moralising. Nevertheless, *Deux ou trois choses* remains a sumptuous and forceful film opening out onto the great ambiguities.

Having explored the theme of prostitution with him, I reached the end of my association with Godard. My feelings towards him were contradictory. The proletarian myth and the militant cinema haven't added anything to his former seductiveness, and neither have the discreet winks he addressed to the big economic powers. I admire him, from a distance. But I never forgot the fundamentals: his courageous and brilliant independence and the instinctive friendship I feel for my old associate.

In the beginning, ambiguity was his forte. He left it behind in favour of terseness. Today, he is coming back to it in order to dispel his illusions. I still expect from him my best moments of cinema. . . .

NOTE

1. ['Sous le pavé de la plage' presents an untranslatable pun evoking both the May '68 slogan 'Under the pavement, the beach' and a publicity poster of the beach.]

Paris, 2 September 1964

Dear Jean-Luc Godard,

Although I am weary of the use of quotations in the cinema, for which unfortunately you will find thousands of opportunities in D.A.F. de Sade, please accept *La philosophie dans le boudoir* as a travelling companion. This edition was lent to me by a leather-jacketed teenage delinquent who demanded its restitution within three weeks at the very latest. He is likely to carry out his cruel threats should I fail to deliver.

I implore you to watch over this book with the utmost care and to ensure its timely return to Paris.

Yours,

A. Dauman

A R G O S F I L M S

Société à Responsabilité Limitée Capital 50.000 F - R.C. Seine 60 B 3062

4, Rue Duphot - PARIS (ler)

Tél. : OPE 60-90 - RIC 10-04 PARIS, le 4 Jànvier 1965

Monsieur Jean-Luo GODARB
9, rue Toullier
P A R I S (5°)

"AVEC LE SOURIRE"

Cher Monsieur,

Pour répondre favorablement à votre demande et malgré
le préjudice qu'une telle mesure inflige à notre Société,
nous vous donnons notre accord pour reporter dans le
courant de l'année 1965 la date des prises de vues du film
sous rubrique.

Rappelons que, selon vos instructions, nous avons
réglé à Teona une somme de Frs : 5.000.-, montant qui doit
être déduit des versements prévus en votre faveur par
notre contrat du 5 Octobre 1964.

Veuillez avoir l'amabilité de nous retourner deux
exemplaires de la présente revêtus de votre signature
précédée de la mention "LU ET APPROUVE."

Nous vous prions de croire, cher Monsieur, à
l'assurance de nos sentiments les plus fidèles.

A. DAUMAN

lu et approuvé
Jean-Luc Godard

Argos Films
4 rue Duphot
Paris I

Paris, 4 January 1965

M. Jean-Luc GODARD
9, rue Toullier
PARIS V

Re.: *Avec le sourire*

Dear Sir,
   Acceding to your request in spite of the damage it inflicts on our Company, we hereby agree to postpone the shooting of the above-mentioned film until later in 1965.
   We would like to remind you that, as per your instructions, we paid Tecna 5,000 Frs which will have to be deducted from the payments due to you according to our contract of 5 October 1964.
   Please be so kind as to return two copies of this letter duly signed under the phrase 'READ AND APPROVED'.

Yours sincerely,

A. DAUMAN

Read and approved
Jean-Luc Godard

WITH A SMILE [AVEC LE SOURIRE]

A telephone rings. A hand picks it up, brings it to
the ear. We discover the face of Lavinia S., a
beautiful young woman of Roman high society.

   On the telephone, one of her friends asks about
her stay in Paris. Lavinia replies an adventure
happened to her so incredible that she can barely
bring herself to talk about it. She lowers her voice
to tell the following story:

PARIS
A luxurious Lancia stops in front of the iron gate
of an Embassy. On one of its wings there is a small
Italian flag. Inside, a high official of the Italian
government kisses a woman who will go and do some
shopping while he goes to a meeting at the British
Embassy (or some other one).

   The young woman leaves her husband, kisses him
one last time through the lowered window, impas-
sively observed by the driver.

   We have recognised Lavinia S., supremely chic and
elegant. She and her husband are to meet in one hour
at the Ritz Hotel or at the Continental.

   The car drives into the Embassy grounds and now
we follow Lavinia as she wanders along, window
shopping.

   It is a beautiful autumn afternoon, soft and mild,
which makes her look more innocently artless than
ever.

   She looks to the right and to the left, happy to
be alive and to be walking in a Paris so welcoming
to the aimless stroller.

   All of a sudden, she notices a young, fairly pretty
woman on the opposite side of the street, by a window
of a small flat.

   Leaning on the window-sill, the young woman
appears to be watching the spectacle of the street.
Now and then, a furtive smile crosses her face, very
quickly, almost invisible unless you are watching
her closely, as does Lavinia wondering who those
smiles are addressing.

   Suddenly, right after a smile, but without there
even being a noticeable cause and effect connection,
a man stops by the window, then enters the building
by a side door.

   Lavinia then sees the young woman draw the
curtains and close the window. She walks on a bit

but returns to her vantage point and, after a few minutes, she sees the curtains opening and the young woman leaning on the sill again as she starts addressing furtive smiles to passers-by.

Lavinia finally understands that she is a prostitute.

(Lavinia's thoughts could perhaps be written in French on the screen in ornamental letters, translating the Italian voice-off.)

Lavinia is shocked by the nerve of this Parisian woman but at the same time she admires the efficiency of her work.

Lavinia walks along the streets, through the gardens of the Champs-Elysées, lost in her thoughts.

Abruptly, she is struck by an absurd idea. She wonders whether a man would stop in front of her if she were to give him a little smile like the Parisian woman in the window.

The more absurd and dangerous this idea seems, the more Lavinia trembles with a desire to try it out. A number of men pass by but they look awful and she hesitates for quite a while as she leans against a wall. Then, she makes up her mind and smiles, for no more than a quarter of a second, at a passer-by.

He comes to her and asks: Shall I go with you?

The little bit of French she knows doesn't enable her to get rid of the man, who pretends not to understand what she's saying.

Lavinia moves away. He follows her at a distance. She repeats in an incomprehensible mixture of Italian and French that she made a mistake, that it's all a misunderstanding, that he should leave her in peace, etc.

We notice from his replies in correct French that he thinks she is playing a game, which excites him even more.

Lavinia tries to lose him, in vain. In desperation, she goes into a store. He does too. (Various gags to be devised.)

Then Lavinia tries to get a taxi. Undisturbed, the guy gets in with her and sits down next to her.

The taxi stops in front of the Ritz. Lavinia tries to get rid of the guy, saying goodbye to him as if taking leave of a friend and letting him pay the fare while she hurries in to get her key.

But with an unflappable coolness, he manages to join her in the elevator. Unfortunately for her, he brings her a package she had forgotten in the taxi.

She doesn't have the nerve, in front of the page and the lift boy, to tell the odious man to go away. He keeps playing what he takes to be a game on her part.

And so they go into the apartment of Lavinia and her husband across from the Tuileries.

There, Lavinia bursts into tears and, with the aid of a dictionary, she explains what really happened.

She even offers to pay him to get out because her husband is due to come back in about three quarters of an hour and he is sure to kill her if he finds another man with his wife.

But the guy holds his ground. He understands Lavinia's position very well. It's unfortunate but it doesn't change anything. He doesn't want any money. On the contrary, he is quite prepared to give her money because he fully intends to f... her.

From that point onwards, the second part of the film veers off into a different direction; we abandon Lubitsch and his cigar.

The principle is this:

The guy says he'll go away if Lavinia gives him a kiss. Then he wants two. Then he wants a photographic souvenir, showing her partly undressed.

The guy accompanies his actions with philosophic theories.

In the end, afraid that her husband is about to come back, Lavinia gives in totally to the man's whims.

ROME

Totally? asks the voice of Lavinia's Roman friend on the phone.

Yes, totally, replies Lavinia with that characteristic gesture Italians have to express the obvious.

Jean-Luc Godard

Jean-Luc Godard and Anatole Dauman at a press conference

PREFACE TO 'MASCULIN-FÉMININ'

Chronicle of a Winter

Having spent a lovely May with Marker, then a summer with Rouch which was certainly less extraordinary than Barnet's[1] but nonetheless decisive concerning the relations between cinema and truth, I found myself alone in Paris, in December 1965, in between two rounds of the elections.

I was like that character described by Giraudoux, I think it was in *Palais de glace*, who comes back from the war and finds that all the friends of his age have been killed or have disappeared. By accident, he takes up with a group of youngsters who make an exception and accept him as one of them even though he is ten years older. About the same time, he also bumps into some friends of his father who also make an exception, accepting him as one of them even though he is ten years younger.

And so, like that man from Giraudoux, I found myself navigating between two generations as Siegfried and Simon did between two wars, or like Jérôme[2] between two continents, which is the same thing.

My juniors were a little pop singer who forbade her maid to listen to Radio Luxemburg while she did the dishes because it interfered with her productivity; a young trade unionist who at times was made to deviate from his hard line by sex; a descendant of Werther who felt a little lost between the Blacks and Vietnam, and others who were strange precisely because of being 'others'.

My elders were the world of cinema and its techniques, its languages, so diverse and so contradictory, from Lumière to the young Czech school.

And I felt very much at ease with both, but separately. I wanted them to meet, to make links like Saint-Exupéry's fox,[3] but I was always forced to see them separately, to provide a voice-over commentary to images and faces that should have been able to speak for themselves right away, and on the contrary, to take my distance when a live conversation lacked an explanatory commentary, which shouldn't have been the case either.

So I spent two winter months describing, on the basis of a few specific facts, fifteen to be precise, youth by way of the cinema, unless it was the other way around.

And having on occasion succeeded in getting my elders and my juniors together, I found myself alone, one January morning, far from the youngsters and from the cinema. What remains is a film, an always incomplete dossier, that is to say, incessantly to be completed, which is why you then start on another one.

Jean-Luc Godard

NOTES

1. [References to Chris Marker's *Le joli mai*, Jean Rouch's *Chronique d'un été* and Boris Barnet's comedy *Schedroye Leto* [*A Bountiful Summer*] (1951), released in France as *Un été prodigieux*.]
2. [Characters from Jean Giraudoux' novels *Simon le Pathétique* (1926), *Siegfried et le Limousin* (1922) and *Aventures de Jérôme Bardini* (1930).]
3. [In *Le Petit Prince* (1943).]

MASCULINE AND FEMININE

Script

SEQUENCE 1
Café on the Place Montparnasse, afternoon.
A few customers.
  Dialogue Paul/Madeleine (he barely knows her. One of his friends, Robert, told him she knew a boy who worked on a newspaper where Paul might find some work as he is fed up with the factory).
  Outside, a couple is having a row on the pavement (he or she gets out a gun and shoots the other who falls to the ground).
  A boy comes and joins Madeleine who leaves with him.

SEQUENCE 2
Some café, morning.
  Workers take their morning break.
  Dialogue Paul/Robert by the bar over coffee and croissants. A young woman is drinking coffee next to them.
  Robert amuses himself brushing his elbow against her breasts without her noticing.
  He and Paul do the same with another woman in the street.

SEQUENCE 3
Paul in the editorial office of the journal where he has found work. He is sorting papers and photographs.
  He passes by Madeleine in one of the offices. She is in discussion with her friends, one of them being Catherine, who are about to go shopping.
  Paul takes the opportunity of Madeleine's visit to the lavatory to follow her. He waits for her and when she comes out and washes her hands, he asks whether she would accept him courting her or some such thing.

SEQUENCE 4
After dinner, Paul goes along with Robert who accompanies his father and two or three others to write political slogans on the walls.
  In a beatnik bar where they pause for a drink, Paul notices Catherine and another girl, Élisabeth. They are waiting for Madeleine, who has had a row

with her parents and is moving in with Catherine
and Élisabeth.

Paul persuades Robert to stay and follow the three
girls. He proposes, unsuccessfully, that Madeleine
move in to his spare room rather than to Élisabeth
and Catherine's flat. Madeleine refuses.

As the girls live alongside the elevated section
of the metro, Paul and Robert travel in the metro
to see if they can get a look at them through the
window while they are undressing. They take two or
three return journeys but with no success.

In the compartment, they witness a violent
argument between a black man and a white woman,
ending in a crime.

SEQUENCE 5
Paul has something important to say to Madeleine,
who doesn't have the time because she has an
appointment to make her first record. Paul asks only
for a few minutes in some quiet place. They go into
a café, but every time they sit down, the conversation of the people next to them bothers Paul. In
the end, Madeleine can't stay any longer because
she is late already. Parting from her in front of
the building where she is to make the record, Paul
asks her to marry him.

SEQUENCE 6
Madeleine's performance as a singer in the Locomo-
tive, under the Moulin-Rouge. Paul is there with
Catherine and Élisabeth. He is indignant at Madeleine making a spectacle of herself.

He goes to wait for her, alone, outside. In the
street, he notices a young woman, dropped by another
woman in a car, who seems to be waiting for
something.

SEQUENCE 7
Dialogue Paul/Robert in a launderette.

SEQUENCE 8
Paul is listening to music, late at night, in the
flat of Madeleine's friends. The last metro has gone
and since Paul lives on the other side of Paris,
Madeleine suggests he spend the night with her and
Élisabeth together in the big bed while Catherine
sleeps in the single bed.

Paul and Élisabeth's hands meet and avoid each other
on Madeleine's body, who ends up preferring Paul.

SEQUENCE 9
A brasserie.
    Dialogue Paul/Madeleine as they are eating.
    Next to them, a dialogue between a prostitute and a German tourist.
    Élisabeth joins them.
    A guy, at the table opposite, explains to an actress how she should act in the play she is doing.

SEQUENCE 10
Paul, Madeleine and Élisabeth go to the cinema one Sunday afternoon.
    Paul goes to the gents. He sees two guys kissing. He returns to Madeleine and Élisabeth in the auditorium and obtains Élisabeth's permission to sit between the two of them. Madeleine tells him the beginning of the film, which he missed.
    Paul goes to the projection booth to complain about the film not being projected in the right ratio.
    They leave shortly before the end of the film and Paul has the usher tell him the ending.

SEQUENCE 11
Swedish film to be inserted in sequence 10.

SEQUENCE 12
Dialogue Catherine/Paul while they wait for Madeleine who is finishing a song in a recording studio.
    Catherine and Paul accompany Madeleine to Europe 1 Midi where she is to be interviewed.

SEQUENCE 13
On top of a building under construction.
    Paul shows Madeleine where his future flat will be, bought with money inherited from his grandparents.
    Élisabeth accompanies them and has a row with Paul, who refuses to let her come and live there as well as Madeleine.
    Paul misses his footing, falls and is killed. Élisabeth consoles Madeleine.

Masculin-féminin

Antoine Bourseiller and Brigitte Bardot in Masculin-féminin

```
Anouchka Films
Argos Films       Paris                    Masculin

Svensk Filmindustri                        Féminin
Sandrews   Stockholm
```

SUMMARY

```
I    - Manuscript - Music                     33,500
II   - Technical crew and labour             200,900
III  - Cast                                   38,300
IV   - Decors                                 25,000
V    - Shooting equipment                     13,400
VI   - Electrical equipment                    7,000
VII  - Stock and processing                   74,530
VIII - Sound-tracks and editing               25,050
IX   - Expenses and transport - Production    58,000
X    - Miscellaneous-costumes-publicity       18,000
XI   - Insurance                              20,000
XII  - Social insurance and tax               55,000
                                             568,680


       Contingency and general expenses       31,320


                                             600,000
```

```
Paris, 12.11.65
```

SAVATE[1] AND FINANCE
OR TWO OR THREE THINGS I KNOW ABOUT HIM

Why did I join the producers of *Deux ou trois choses
que je sais d'elle*? Is it because Jean-Luc has been
a friend of mine for nigh on twenty years or because
Godard is the greatest film-maker in the world?

Jean-Luc Godard is not the only one who films as
he breathes, but he is the one who breathes best.
He is quick like Rossellini, wicked like Sacha
Guitry, musical like Orson Welles, simple like
Pagnol, hurt like Nicholas Ray, effective like
Hitchcock, profound, profound, profound like Ingmar
Bergman and insolent like nobody else.

Even those who hate Godard, sitting in the dark
before one of his films, well, even if they don't
understand a thing, I guarantee you that they won't
miss a beat. In other words, just as the O.R.T.F.
examines audience ratings, you could measure the
intensity in an auditorium while a Godard film is
being projected and you would find that he knows
how to make himself heard and watched like nobody
else.

He is the one who killed off the two or three
worst things I know about the public: polite

Jean-Pierre Léaud and Chantal Goya in Masculin-féminin

indifference, vague interest, amused condescension. His authority, since that is what we are talking about, is such that you might call it a good-luck charm or an *infallibility* curse. Will Jean-Luc Godard become more popular than the Pope, that is to say, just a little less than the Beatles? It's possible. Professor Chiarini has stated: 'There is the cinema *pre*-Godard and *post*-Godard.' That's true, and as the years go by we grow more certain that *A bout de souffle* (1960) marked a crucial turning point in the cinema just as *Citizen Kane* did in 1940. Godard has pulverised the system, he has turned the cinema inside out just as Picasso did in painting, and like him, he has made everything possible. France, formerly called Gaul, is turning into a country with a population of forty-five million cineastes. Filming from morning till night, it is a real pleasure to see him and to act as the financier of such a brilliant 'savate fighter'.

More soberly, I can conclude by saying that I became the coproducer of Jean-Luc Godard's thirteenth film because I noticed that the people who invested money in his twelve previous masterpieces have all become rich.

François Truffaut

NOTE

1. [La Savate is a French type of foot-boxing.]

JEAN-LUC GODARD IN DISCUSSION WITH FRANÇOIS CHÂTELET

François Châtelet: What do you think of the provocative synopsis of your film?
Jean-Luc Godard: A synopsis only concerns the viewer. In fact, I didn't want to signify anything, and Vietnam is present by definition, not because of the way the script is constructed.

FC: Your last films appear to go in a new direction. Some people – I am not one of them – might find them more 'committed', more realistic, and could consider them to be a systematic depiction presenting and redoubling the human condition caught in industrial civilisation. How do you see your own activity and your evolution?
JLG: You know, when someone behind the wheel of a car poses himself questions, that's called driving, and when Picasso does, that's called painting. Me, I film, that is to say, I put things in front of cameras . . . or cameras in front of things. Filming is a way of life, like boxing is to a boxer. If I couldn't shoot any more, oh well, I would do something else. I would go to the cinema more often! I would write criticism. It may be rather like a moral attitude. I don't know why people are so down on morality. That must be because we confuse it with the kind of gesticulation that simulates it precisely where it is absent. Morality is to look for a truth, something you can say clearly and that will satisfy. My films, then, are 'essays'. Yes, that's it: I am an essayist with a camera.

FC: A critical essayist.
JLG: A self-critical one. But in self-criticism there is criticism. The modern novel is always at the same time a novel and a search for an answer to questions such as: 'Why write?', 'What is writing?' And painting too conveys an anxiety about the empty canvas and about the meaning of the act of painting. It is the same in the cinema. 'Why does this shot stop here rather than there?' 'Why show this rather than that?' You want a complete object but you never get anything but silhouettes.

FC: Any determination is a negation! But I wanted to hear you clarify the way you conceive of this critical activity, in the political sense of the

term, which your films seem to aim for. There we
find obsessions about Vietnam, the Ben Barka affair,
China and, in this case, social prostitution.
JLG: If you want to say something, there is only
one thing to be done: say it. Vietnam is something
I want to talk about, so I talk about it. It is the
same with the word 'communist'. You hardly ever hear
it in other films. So I like it to be heard. In
fact, that isn't just a matter of politics, it is
also aesthetic. These are images (sound or graphic
images) that have a mysterious beauty in themselves.
My last film doesn't actually tell you about
prostitution, but that is its truth. The truth of
our world is prostitution. Advertising? Prostitution! Writing? Prostitution! Even making films!
Capitalism is that. And it is a sickness that is
easily exported. I just came back from Algeria. I
found a fascinating audience there, young and with
little education, but who could experience the
fascination of the images as such. On the other
hand, in the world of the cinema, you can feel very
strongly (already or still!) the hold of capitalism.
So, the prostitutes of these large entities are
people who, like anybody else, want to possess
objects which are regarded as being the precondition
of happiness!

FC: If I were to play devil's advocate and accuse
you of being provocative, what would you say? Because
your attitude – for instance about the Chinese
cultural revolution – puts one in mind of the cheek
of the surrealists who wanted to see the Cossacks
water their horses at the fountain of the Place de
la Concorde.
JLG: In our society, people no longer know how to
say yes or no (leaving aside dictated referenda).
All we can say is maybe. The sleepers must be woken
up. What is happening in China, and I recognise its
caricatural aspects, is very interesting. It may be
the beginning of a big tremor, the end of the Big
Sleep laying in wait for us.

FC: In your film, all the dialogues have been
borrowed from a patchwork of texts. One gets the
impression that you, as a collector of spectacles
and of spectacular sentences, are collaging fragments of reality together as if you were playing
with a Meccano set. Would you say that in a world
saturated with language one cannot 'speak' any more,

only recompose? Or is it to convey the bric-à-brac nature of the sound of the world we live in?

JLG: You work with the pieces reality gives you. I like to think that I am a *worker* (that's a term I found in Macherey's book).[1] I make something that is 'me' and 'independent of me' at the same time. Some of my 'effects' emerge in the 'manufacturing' process. Isn't that the case with an artisan? He has an idea of the whole but as far as the details are concerned, he lets himself be guided by the grain of the wood. I also like to compare myself to a mathematician. When I was at school, I wanted to do mathematics, or rather, I dreamt that I wanted to do that. What attracted me was the idea of doing pure research . . . What I'm telling you isn't very coherent: a worker who makes a material object and a mathematician who only deals with pure abstractions! Although, on second thoughts, the two aren't incompatible! They adjust to each other, they are productive without having to appeal to some mystical inspiration!

FC: I think that throughout your work the notion of a revolutionary art has found a new or a renewed meaning. Surrealism and its watered-down offshoots have shown up the limits purely formal revolutions come up against. Socialist realism is just bureaucratic idiocy. Whether art repeats itself in the bourgeois manner or in the socialist manner, it is just as boring. When it prophesies or moralises, it is no longer art. Among the various roads open to you, you have found the one which is effectively and radically critical in that it leaves nothing in place: neither what you speak about nor how you speak nor, finally, you who are speaking. What do you want from the viewer?

JLG: He is in front of a film: let him look. Everything in it consists of images, including the sounds, the sentences. He should make the best of it! In a film, perception is the activity of thought. You are not dealing with a speech.

Interview for *La Quinzaine littéraire*,
15 March 1967

NOTE

1. [Pierre Macherey was Professor of Philosophy and a close associate of Louis Althusser; author of *Pour une théorie de la production littéraire*, Paris, 1966, translated as *A Theory of Literary Production*, Routledge & Kegan Paul, London, 1978.]

Filming Deux ou trois choses .

FAITHFUL JORIS

Joris Ivens, the giant of the documentary cinema, object of general admiration, finds in me a passionate lover of his images and a severe censor of his evangelism. However, I gladly acknowledge that his linguistic mannerisms or his ready-made revolutionary thinking don't seem to shock many people. I'm surprised and I compliment him.

Joris Ivens. (Above) *Filming* 17th Parallel

A Valparaiso *by Joris Ivens*

OUR FRIEND VOLKER

Volker Schlöndorff has been my companion since way back. In 1966, I discovered *Young Törless* at the Cannes Festival and found it gripping. It is one of his best films even though Volker was only twenty-six years old. . . .

My friend Volker came to France to finish his studies and to get into the cinema in the traditional way via the Institut des hautes études cinémato-graphiques and an assistant directorship. On the set of *Marienbad*, Resnais had just introduced his first assistant to me, Jean Léon, when suddenly he turned towards this young man with a shaven head, saying: 'This is my other first assistant, and when I say "first" I mean first.' Resnais' words being The Word, I looked more closely at the incumbent of this newly created post, 'the second-first assistant ex aequo'.

As life hadn't arranged to make our paths cross, I didn't hear anything from Volker for a few years, until the day I accepted an invitation from Benalmadena's Festival of Authors' Films, which was organising a tribute to me. A long time ago I had glimpsed something of Andalusia in Roger Vadim's *Les Bijoutiers du clair de lune* (1957), but I didn't know that since then a concrete wall had been erected there, barely sparing Malaga, the gardens of the Puerta Oscura and its horse-drawn carriages. I came out of a screening of Volker's film *Strohfeuer* all aglow. It showed a striking intuitive grasp of the behind the scenes world of women, rather like in Bergman. 'Throughout the film,' Volker confided, 'I felt penetrated by a woman.' This robust way of putting it revealed the extent of his collaboration with Margarethe von Trotta, his wife. For the first time, her name appeared as co-scenarist. Soon she would be co-director and then full-time director. A remarkable development of the transmission of a woman's look!

About fifty journalists were waiting for Volker's press conference. At that time, in 1972, some people were haunted by memories of May 68. Out of the blue, Volker referred to the theory according to which a film's artistic value is necessarily corrupted by its theatrical distribution, the degree of corruption being in proportion to the number of spectators. Underneath this exalted profession of faith, I distinctly felt a kind of suicidal aspiration, a will towards imprisonment in the margins by a generous man who wanted to open himself to any and all experiences. I guessed there was a fatal relationship between the feminine feeling that pervaded his film and the spider's strategy subtly attracting him towards the joys of damnation. Fortunately, Volker subsequently came to desire an independent existence, which allowed him to achieve immense successes with mainstream audiences.

Volker Schlöndorff

It was in Benalmadena that Volker told me about his intention to adapt Marguerite Yourcenar's *Le Coup de grâce*. He asked me to help him to realise this old dream by securing the rights to the book. I immediately agreed to this Franco-German co-production project, although observing with some amusement: 'Don't you think Mme Yourcenar is a little too academic for someone like you?'

The novel, set in the aftermath of World War I, is well known. In the film, absolute respect for historical detail and a faultless inspiration combine to make *Le Coup de grâce* one of the great achievements of a cineaste who embodies the renewal of the German cinema. The film first opened in Germany, in Munich, where Margarethe von Trotta, the co-writer of the adaptation as well as the lead actress, delivered herself of numerous pronouncements underlining the 'class struggle' aspect of the film. If you check with Marguerite Yourcenar's preface and with the recollections of *Bajazet*, the Racine tragedy she explicitly uses as a reference, that interpretation seems exceedingly far-fetched. It cannot be denied that a Racinian spirit pervades the novel and that nothing in the film itself authorises such a sociological reading. This blundering crypto-Marxist launch effectively killed the film's chances in a divided Germany.

Consequently, I took precautions for the French premiere in Biarritz. I advised Volker by phone that my anti-aircraft artillery installed along the Rhine had orders to shoot down the plane carrying Margarethe von Trotta should she decide to come and lend her support to my promotional campaign. I even managed to convince Volker to insert, before the End credit, the last lines of the novel. This is where Eric, Sophie's lover, despairingly speaks the lines that remove any trace of doubt about the heroine's real motives: 'At first I thought that in asking me to become an executioner, she had intended to give me a final proof of her love, the most conclusive proof of all. But I understood afterwards that she only wished to take revenge, leaving me prey to remorse. She was right in her calculations: I do feel remorse at times. One is always trapped, somehow, in dealings with women.'

Predictably, France was the only country where *Le Coup de grâce* became a major critical success.

In 1980, the Cultural Affairs people at the Quai d'Orsay urged me to give a series of lectures in the Levant. Together with M. de Galard, our pleasant cultural adviser, I went to the cinémathèque of Istanbul. The Turkish left, extremely thick on the ground in these small venues, had come to see the famous *Coup de grâce*, which was preceded by 'Trottist' pronouncements. I started my talk with some rhetorical questions which obviously would be in the minds of this attentive intelligentsia: 'Does this film illustrate the theory according to which, at a specific point in history, a fraction of the ruling class comes to support the aspirations of the proletariat's avant-garde? Isn't it true that our heroine exemplifies the revolutionary action that a member of the aristocracy can and must engage in if she wants to free herself from the alienation of her class?'

Having thus secured the general goodwill and approval of my audience, I began to criticise the basis of the Leninist exegeses propagated by the two authors

Le Coup de grâce *(Margarethe von Trotta)*

Anatole, quelle voie m'indiquer- tu ?

'Anatole, which direction are you pointing me in?': Volker Schlöndorff with Anatole Dauman

of the film. I suggested a double explanation founded on a reading of the second preface to *Bajazet*, a text Marguerite Yourcenar herself had pointed to as her main source of inspiration. Why had Marguerite Yourcenar chosen to locate the action of her novel in the Baltic countries in 1919? For the same reason, I explained, that Racine had chosen Constantinople as the location for his tragedy: heroes inspire more respect the further they are removed from ordinary mortals. Reading from the book, I quoted the extracts from Racine which Marguerite Yourcenar had used in the preface to her novel: 'It is as if our respect for heroes increases the further they are removed from us (. . .) The remoteness of countries compensates in a way for too close a proximity in time. Because to ordinary people, it makes little difference whether something is, so to speak, a thousand years removed or a thousand miles distant.' By removing them in space to the outer edges of Europe, I continued, the heroes of *Coup de grâce*, caught in the lethal games of passion, come close to those of antiquity, those of *Memoirs of Hadrian*, that other admirable book by Marguerite Yourcenar. As they followed the thread of my argument, the audience was bemused and lost track of its familiar political points of reference. This allowed me to dish out *Coup de grâce*'s abrupt truth to them: a monstrous love with no way out! Only our friendly cultural adviser seemed to appreciate that peremptory conclusion. Racine and Lacan had the same effect in Constantinople as Lenin had in Munich.

'Anatole, this is where you've led me . . . Thanks. Volker Schlöndorff'

But how would the film do, flanked by its double exegesis, in that temple of the Ponant[1] which was Filmex, the big film festival of the American West Coast? After the press conference, Billy Wilder, who thought highly of Schlöndorff, invited us out to dinner. Did the old director, at ease in his glorious reputation, want to designate a putative heir to whom he could entrust the status of Austrian cinema in Hollywood? We went to a restaurant owned by Billy Wilder, unbeknownst to everyone. I entered a place that left me speechless. Was I at Lipp's or at Maxim's? Wilder explained that I was looking at the set for *Irma la Douce* (1963), designed by Alexandre Trauner. As soon as we sat down, he punchily launched into an ironic conversation:

Wilder: Do you think you're going to make money with your film? If the story of a film is complicated, its background has to be simple. If the background is complicated, the story must be simple. But both at the same time, that will never work, I can tell you that for sure! Schlöndorff, you worked hard on this; six months shooting, probably. And you, Mr Dauman, you must have sunk one or two million dollars into this business. And all that for peanuts.

Dauman: There is one question that's been bothering me for nigh on twenty-five years. From the first image of *Sunset Boulevard*, you can see the corpse of a man floating in a swimming pool. He is the one who is about to tell us the story of his life in the first person. How can a dead man tell us the story of his life?

Wilder: The version that was released to the public wasn't what I wanted to do initially. In the first version, the film had a pre-credits sequence in the Beverly Hills morgue. An employee was completing the administrative formalities; he took a stamp and stamped the big toe of a young man. In voice off, you could hear the boy tell of his last moments. Then the employee approaches an old man who is heard describing the circumstances of his own death. That sequence ended with the corpse of William Holden, whose voice informed the viewers that all his life he had dreamt of a swimming pool. The next shot showed the corpse drifting in the water and everybody could understand what was happening. But I had to cut the morgue scenes because during a preview, some people in the audience started to laugh. That taught me a lesson.

Dauman: What do you mean? Some people laugh and you are supposed to change your work? Were you a victim of the awful 'final cut' rule?

Wilder: My dear fellow, it's very simple. I approve of previews. If you ignore the reactions of the audience, there is no way you can exercise your profession properly.

That was the view of this Hollywood giant, respectful of the laws laid down by the audience. I owed it to myself to offer some sort of defence of the European cinema: *Le Coup de grâce* hadn't been shot in six months, as would have been the case in America, but in five or six weeks. I hadn't invested one million dollars, let alone two, because the budget had been kept below 400,000 dollars. In Europe, professional and public funds were available to support production. And above all, France didn't apply the law of the final cut and we were relatively independent of the public. Billy Wilder changed the subject and entertained us for the rest of the dinner with that mordant wit that endows all his films with an eternal youthfulness.

Le Coup de grâce was released in New York in the middle of a snow storm. The cinema was excellent, but the inclement weather got the better of some spectators who had thought of going there . . .

NOTE

1. [Echoing the notion of The Levant for the Orient, the Ponant refers to the Occident.]

Petite Plaisance
Northeast Harbor
Maine 04662

To Volker Schlöndorff
Obermaierstrasse 1
8 Munich 22
Federal Germany   12 July 1976

Dear Sir,

Thank you for your letter of 21 June. I find it most interesting that your work should have led you to centre the film more on Sophie. In my view, critics have all too often neglected her character in favour of Eric. It rather brings to mind Pirandello's six characters competing for the lead.

I am not planning to go to New York in the coming months.

Again I wish you every success.

Kindest regards to both you and Margarethe von Trotta.

Marguerite Yourcenar

Volker Schlöndorff's The Tin Drum

VOLKER SCHLÖNDORFF

(Extracts from 'My Diary of *Die Blechtrommel* [*The Tin Drum*]')

Early in 1977 I went on two long journeys: one to the West, to California, Hollywood; the other to the East, through Moscow to Central Asia, Tashkent. In Hollywood, I had discussions about projects that were offered to me following the success of *Katharina Blum*, projects for so-called 'international' films. Margarethe von Trotta, Martje and Werner Herzog and I had seen our films with the eyes of Uzbeks. After this pendular swing from East to West, I was more determined than ever to remain centred in my own place, despite the possibilities elsewhere, despite the difficulties here. Since *Törless*, I have deliberately and consciously made German films.

When I had clarified my geographical and historical point of view, Franz Seitz brought me *Die Blechtrommel*.

In the fifties, when Grass was writing the book in Paris, I was preparing my French 'baccalauréat' only a few houses away, but I was so deeply immersed in France that I didn't read the novel.

23 April 1977
Today read *Die Blechtrommel* for the first time and tried to imagine the film that could be made from it. It could become a very German fresco, the history of the world seen and experienced from below: enormous, spectacular paintings grouped together by the tiny Oskar.

It has been said that he is a creation of the twentieth century. To me he possesses two typically contemporary qualities: rejection and protest.

He rejects the world to the point of not growing up. Zero growth.

He protests so loudly that his voice shatters glass. Seen in this light, he is even closer to us now than fifteen years ago, when the book came out.

I feel that the possibility of working on *Die Blechtrommel* is a challenge I can't possibly refuse. So, I accept it without having the slightest idea of how to set about it. I suppose it will go on for several years. For that very reason, I have no hesitation in allowing myself to be carried away.

30 June 1977
Franz Seitz and I visit Günter Grass for the first time. He has cooked lentils with bacon for us. We

immediately come to the point. *Die Blechtrommel* is
the opposite of a *Bildungsroman*: everything and
everyone develops around Oskar, except himself.
Oskar portrays the thirst for revenge of the lower
middle class, its anarchistic dreams of grandeur.
Günter Grass explains the significance of objects,
which sometimes provide the decision for action, as
in the Nouveau Roman: the drum, the clock, the game
of Skat, the necklace, the Party badge.

   Despite a lively conversation, we remain stran-
gers. The dimensions of the task make me panic and
I am terrified by the author. Most of the things in
the book that one takes to be the fruit of
imagination is for him experienced reality. Oskar
mustn't be filmed literature. Not only does Grass
contradict the notion that one can no longer write
novels but the stories crowd in on him as lived
experiences that must be communicated. Where, in
the film, will this inner sense of energy come from?

July 1977
After a first draft using flashbacks, I try to tell
Oskar's adventures chronologically. Only a selection of a few typical scenes. Refusal of plenitude;
remain within the time period between birth and the
end of the war. The post-war period would be a second
film, with another actor; work for later on.

   I stick to childhood; look for the Oskar in me.
My films are only good when I can identify with the
characters. Read a great deal about Danzig, the
petit bourgeoisie and the Nazis: newspapers, novels,
documents.

August 1977
The size of the project causes not only narrative
difficulties but production problems as well. We
get in touch with American distributors. I leave
for Paris. Several times I try to tell the story of
Die Blechtrommel in production offices. 'Tell me
the story in three lines.' I don't yet have what
constitutes the book's real substance: Günter Grass'
language. In spite of chaotically translated notes,
the power of the story comes across, the moving and
contradictory figure of Oskar Matzerath fascinates.
I become more confident about the possibility of
making the film.

25 August 1977
The decisive moment, last night at Jean-Claude

Carrière's place. We hadn't seen each other since
Viva Maria, thirteen years ago. I told him of my
difficulties and especially what Bertrand Tavernier
had told me over lunch: a film with a dwarf as the
central character reduces everything to dwarves'
problems.

Jean-Claude reassures me. The key word is *The Kid*.
We need a Jackie Coogan. Everybody can identify with
a child. It won't be a film about a dwarf but a film
about childhood.

28 August 1977
I go to Normandy especially to meet Anatole Dauman,
my co-producer on *Le Coup de grâce*. I know he doesn't
like relying on scripts, preferring to listen to
directors and to discuss their project with them.
For two long afternoons, I tell him the story, with
the novel and my notes in my hand, scene by scene,
of my *Blechtrommel*. He only has a vague memory of
Grass' novel. A priori, the idea of making such an
important film without big stars appears odd to him.
But little by little the story excites him. By the
time I get to the end of Oskar's adventures, the
decision has been taken: he will be the French
co-producer. To start with, he hires Jean-Claude
Carrière to write the script with me. So, the
kick-off took place in Honfleur . . .

Jean-Claude Carrière will work with me from
October onwards, when he will be finished with
Buñuel. Saw many films before leaving Paris. Nothing
that could come even near to *Die Blechtrommel*.

20 September 1977
Went with Franz Seitz to the Congress of Small People
at Goslar. About sixty dwarves in the Imperial
castle. Oskar cannot be a dwarf, he must be a child.
Otherwise, the film becomes a film about the problem
of dwarves.

1 October 1977
I have written a first draft; chronological; almost
no dialogue, no commentary. Jean-Claude Carrière
arrives in Munich. We start writing the script,
scene by scene, following my outline.

20 October 1977
There is something rough about *Die Blechtrommel*,
like a rough wood engraving; often it is almost
gross. The equivalent in cinema would be the early

Chaplin. Oskar is also *The Kid*. This continual revolt
of the child against the world of grown-ups. Very
ordinary situations, like in a boxing match, where
people can shout and boo from the audience. The
opposite of a 'literary adaptation', often barbarous
in the sense that Glauber Rocha gives to that word
when talking about Latin American films.

We don't always succeed in getting under Oskar's
skin. Just as he speaks of himself at times in the
first person, at times in the third person – with
a childlike distance – the narration must at times
be completely subjective and at times must show him
from the outside, with a sense of dread. As it is
impossible anyway to recreate the entire book, I am
concentrating more and more on a few big scenes,
almost like music hall numbers.

15 November 1977
The Hessische Rundfunk will be co-producer.

20 November 1977
Paris/London. Production problems. We interrupt the
work on the script. Minimum cost of the film as we
want to make it: 6.7 million Marks. It seems as
impossible to finance a German film of that dimension
as it would be to recover the cost. Among the
American distributors, United Artists seems interested. Discussions in Paris and in London; can *Die
Blechtrommel* be transformed into an international
film by way of an international cast?

Maybe Roman Polanski or Dustin Hoffman as Oskar,
Isabelle Adjani and Keith Carradine as the parents?
We soon agree: the star of the film is its subject.
The more authentic our representation, the more
exciting the film will be. So, no stars, no
Anglo-American version. German and Polish actors
and a boy of twelve in the lead role. That is the
only way to make *Die Blechtrommel*. I show stills of
little David who is taking a drum course at the
Munich Opera.

1 December 1977
This decision, taken unanimously by all those
involved, nevertheless proves to be incompatible
with all the commercial considerations. So, taking
the risks into account, all participants put a limit
on their investment. Half the money is still missing.

15 December 1977
We do not submit the script to the Projects Fund

today, because the fund must have been spent for 1977. Let's wait until next year.

January 1978
Angela Winkler will play Oskar's mother, Mario Adorf his father.

13 February 1978
Spent three days with Jean-Claude Carrière at Grass's. He called our script 'Protestant and Cartesian'. He misses the irrational irruption of time, the nodal points where everything clashes and breaks down in an irrational and tragicomic manner. On the one hand he asks for more hard realism, and on the other more courage to be unreal. Imagination as a part of the real – Oskar's reality. Those few points are enough to set us working on a new version. The detour through the linear outline proves to have been very useful. We are far removed from the novel, we have an autonomous narrative structure for the film; now we can complete it, destroy it and bring it to life again.

Two journeys to Gdansk further remove us from literature and bring us closer to reality. We start looking for the novel's locations which have almost all been preserved. How small and narrow everything is; one glance is enough to take in the whole suburb between the railway and the tramway. A church, a school, the brasserie, a few shops . . .

To Oskar, this microcosm is the whole world. But to transpose this into images, it isn't enough to film the area as it was (or still is); we have to compose the images that impose themselves in the reading. A re-memorised Danzig, evoked through signs.

26 February 1978
Voyages to Lübeck and to Copenhagen, possible locations for Danzig, and to Yugoslavia, location recces in Zagreb for the crowd scenes and for the Polish postal office.

1 March 1978
In Geneva, saw Daniel Olbrychski on the stage. He will play Jan Bronski, Oskar's second father, the Pole.

The Project Fund (RFA) delays its decision about our project to its next meeting – if there still is one, because the law that set up the fund is coming to the end of its life. In any case, nothing new before the end of May. The city of Berlin announces a credit plan for cinema. Nobody knows when it will come into operation because the basic outline of the plan hasn't been agreed yet. We have to postpone shooting from May to August.

April 1978
Telephone call from Warsaw. We can use the Gdansk locations as Danzig.

1 May 1978
Casting finished: Ferreol and Aznavour are added. But we can't sign the contracts because there is no money.

14 May 1978
A new visit to Grass, almost a year after the first one. This time with a finished script. Now it is 'more Catholic' and less rational, also much bigger – a film of almost two and a half hours. Once again we re-work the dialogue, which amuses both of us. Without it being a comedy, it is very funny. No more distrust of the film-maker, no more fear of the author. A year's work has brought us together. 'Next time we will write an original script straight away,' Grass says as we part.

2 June 1978
Return to Gdansk and to Warsaw, this time with the Polish crew. We talk about *Die Blechtrommel* amongst the Germans, the Poles and especially the Kashubes, because our assistant director Andrej is a Kashub. They are very interested in the project. What to us is a long repressed past is still very topical to them. Our journey is often more like a diplomatic mission than the preparation of a film. A great deal of reality imposes itself, in particular in discussions with the Polish actors.

5 June 1978
Warsaw: Franz Seitz calls me from Munich. Berlin has granted us the loan: we can sign the contract with Poland.

12 June 1978
Today, the Project Fund has also given its grant. We can start: tomorrow, recording of the playback music, next week costume and make-up rehearsals for all the actors. In seven weeks we start shooting!

Nagisa Oshima

THE DIVINE NAGISA

Why did I produce Nagisa Oshima's *Empire of the Senses*? I hesitate to answer because in Eros' company things are never quite completely innocent. But the divine Nagisa has his own utterly simple idea: the guilty one is Dauman.

The cinema of the 70s was beginning to worry about the equivocal aspects of the surge of pornography. Flourishing in the United States, it was getting ready to invade French cinemas. Conformism and the bourgeois fear of sexual provocations were threatening to re-activate the zeal of the institutions charged with the administration of moral well-being. The French political class was obliged to issue a statement about the new freedoms relating to the position of women, the dignity of the individual and other topics of concern to progressive liberalism. In the end, they got lost in the confusion caused by the so-called scandal of cinematic obscenity. So the time had come to affirm the rights of artistic freedom in the domain of the erotic.

Nagisa Oshima's violent and sophisticated art made him a ready-made target for censorship and opprobrium. Oshima had acquired a flattering reputation in Europe thanks to the two films I had made available to Western audiences: *Death by Hanging* and *The Ceremony*. But in Tokyo, where he was regarded as a film master, Oshima thought that his career was doomed: the major companies had no other ambition than to cater to the taste of the teenagers who constituted the bulk of the Japanese audiences.

I felt like taking up the challenge. I could feel the obscurantist wind blowing, threatening to destroy once again the 'flowers of evil'. Artists had to attack if they were to defend themselves. Oshima, following his usual method, thought of making a film based on an actual event. In 1936, a maid at a hostel had killed and emasculated her lover after a whole week of uninterrupted love-making. If I had followed Oshima's initial inspiration, the action would have revolved around the trial of his heroine, a form he had used already for *Death by Hanging*: 'Stick to the representation of a couple drunk with sexual passion,' I told him. And to make sure of being understood, I added: 'Shoot a corrida of love.' I think that was what Oshima in fact really wanted to do in his heart of hearts. But he wasn't saying so. What's more, he was hiding it. That's why Nagisa, in his *Écrits sur le cinéma 1956–1971* (Paris, 1980), mockingly amuses himself by attributing more responsibility to me in the matter than I want to admit to. He teases me with the word 'pornographic' (which never crossed my lips) and paints a picture of me as if I were an American man of action: 'It was the end of the summer of 1972. Coming back from the Venice Festival, where I had presented *Dear Little*

Presentation of Empire of the Senses *at the Cannes festival*

Summer Sister, I stopped off in Paris. In the lobby of a small projection theatre, the Club 70, Dauman suddenly made the following proposition: "Let's co-produce a film together. It will be a pornographic film. As for the content and the organisation of the production, I'm putting myself in your hands entirely. I provide the money and that's all." '

As you can see, the producer's memory and that of the director are out of synch when it comes to recalling where the desire for the 'corrida of love' came from. Is the divine Nagisa the faithful mirror of my unconscious? Was I the one who pushed him towards Eros?

Sometimes you are lucky enough to find amongst your close friends a superior mind who knows you better than you know yourself. Not bothering to flatter your own argument, he goes straight to the point and utters the words that will put you back on the right track and force you to question yourself. In Pierre Legendre, the great Professor of Law, the historian of religion, the eminent Freudian, that dear friend, I found a supreme listener. I submitted the case of the divine Nagisa to him. Was it him, was it me who had instigated the desire for *Empire of the Senses*? Of the producer and the director, who is whose mirror?

Pierre Legendre was kind enough to hold forth on the subject. It is therefore armed with his text that the producer, passionate about the screen, will reply to the director, passionate about the art of loving!

HE WANTED TO SEE THE TRUTH

Eulogy of a Screen Passion

By Pierre Legendre

He wanted to see the truth! May Anatole Dauman receive by way of my notarial pen this tribute in words inspired by our Rimbaud, the author of a notorious tale showing man divided, Prince and Genius intertwined in the Poet, to whom another shattered man, Fernand Léger, devoted an unforgettable drawing. *Through the cinema, illumination!* Such could be Argos' motto, under the sign of the Owl, the bird of mythological Nights.

If you hadn't guessed already, it really is the devil who, through the parade of his Master Jugglers, fires a producer of that calibre, a man tempered by the unyielding toughness of things: the passion of the Mirror, or, as Rimbaud would say, of the magnetic comedy.

A rare event, courtesy of the screen: through men and women artists, creators of tears and laughter, others can enjoy the illusion of living. I mean: a real life, a life that doesn't have to take account of the imperishable, immemorial images of an eternal childhood. Interlacing and tearing asunder, the wind of words gone by, loving to the point of blood: all that ceaselessly keeps forming under the unflinching eye of cameras criss-crossing the planet. Children of the war, all those things have allowed us to survive the imprisonments of the century and will keep our children alive.

Is there a place, in our industrial world ever pushed into tighter concentration, to reflect on *what is a producer*? The question gets lost in the mist if you only consider the massive presence of the dinosaurs, Warner Bros., 20th Century-Fox, etc, those immense factories, impenetrable to ordinary mortals. On the contrary, for an artisan like Dauman, being a producer comes down to this: to make his world, spectators included, go through the door of the possible into the impossible world of the creative wager. A producer is a name. But what is there under this emblematic name which, in the cinematic ceremony, presents the film and then quickly gives way to the boss of the discourse, the director?

Producer. The word has often struck me as

incongruous, almost pataphysical, close to *repro-
ducer*; the fairground may not be all that far away.
I consulted the Latin language, which opened up new
horizons to me. According to the learned exegesis,
the verb 'to produce' is used to mean: to bring into
the world, to lead where one should go, to amuse
and to make last, but also to deploy an army and
even to prostitute. A vast programme.

Artisanal hands, suited to finding artifice: that
is the basis. Proverbially, they must be able to do
everything: to get on with the financial cooks, to
combine tact and bluntness in doing business with
competitors on a planetary scale; above all, to
gauge film people, bring artists where they say they
want to go even though they may be afraid of
encountering the unexpected there: the image of
their desire – an image that is likely to make more
than one of them recoil.

To bring artists where they say they want to go! Pierre Legendre
might have added to his fraternal message: and to make them laugh
about their embarrassment in the face of a project that crushes
them! Because with my producer's roguishness I poked fun at the
divine Nagisa's tragic mask, especially through my natural inclina-
tion to leave him total authorial freedom. For his part, Oshima
made his comment in his writings on cinema:

Throughout the preparations for the project and in
the various discussions I had with him, I gradually
came to understand Dauman's greatness. It comes from
the fact that, having initiated the project in as
unambiguous a manner as possible, he then leaves
the author completely free and entrusts everything
to him. One might conclude that Dauman is a
phlegmatic and lucid businessman, whereas he is
first of all an artist. To tell the truth, I found
it rather embarrassing that he should talk to me
about such a grave and serious project with laughter,
as if it really were a bit of a joke. After he had
made the proposition to me, he looked at me with
his big eyes, with a kind of restrained laughter.
I was disconcerted. In such circumstances, there is
nothing you can do except agree and laugh. I replied
that I wanted to do the film at any price, but I
think my words lacked conviction. By way of an
excuse, I forced myself to laugh but my face couldn't
possibly manage a look of real joy. I laughed rather
awkwardly and adopted an air of modesty. And yet,

as soon as I was back in Japan, I wrote two projects
and sent them to Dauman. One of them was the story
of Abe Sada. Dauman replied immediately: let's go
with Sada.

It was a joy to see the censorship certificate accorded by the Centre
national de la cinématographie and to read the judgments of the
courts in the Federal German Republic and of the State of New
York which caused censorship worldwide to retreat and ensured
the free circulation of *Empire of the Senses*. To win against Reasons
of State is one thing. But to get the divine Nagisa not to flinch from
his desire to film the corrida of love is the greatest satisfaction the
'pornographic' producer could have got!

Extract from a letter from Nagisa Oshima to Anatole Dauman

Tokyo, 10 April 1976

M. Anatole Dauman,
I know you are doing your utmost to find a better
world release for *Empire of the Senses*, for which
I am very grateful. It is thanks to you that it was
possible to make the film and I am truly embarrassed
to have to add to your worries. Fortunately, the
film was able to find extremely good conditions for
its release in Japan. The only problem remaining is
that of censorship, which is actually a rather high
hurdle to cross and we will have to fight it all
the way.
   Our film - your and our film - *Empire of the
Senses*, has to be, I believe, a very effective weapon
in the fight against Franco-Japanese censorship,
against censorship in our two countries. And we must
push further forward, widening the breach opened up
by *Empire of the Senses*.

INTERVIEW WITH NAGISA OSHIMA ON THE RELEASE OF 'EMPIRE OF THE SENSES'

Question: You contemplated calling your film *Corrida of Love* in Japan. Does that mean that you think of it as a killing?
Answer: For a long time I had been thinking of a project inspired by the famous Sada. Anatole Dauman, the producer I admire the most in the world, one day suggested this title which determined the making of the film.

Q.: What relations do you see between physical passion, the joy of sexual pleasure and death?
A.: An indissoluble bond. In the ecstasies of love, don't people cry out: 'I'm dying'?

Q.: Did you think of Georges Bataille, of Antonin Artaud or of Sade, who inevitably comes to mind because of Sada's name?
A.: I am too lazy to have re-read them before writing the script.

Q.: The action of the film is presented as an uninterrupted act of love; only the places where it happens change according to an itinerary which allows the two lovers no respite whatever. We come across twenty different decors in this way, twenty love-rooms, places enclosed like an arena consecrated to a deadly ritual. Do you think, as we do, that your approach is unique?
A.: As you point out so pertinently, I want the gestures and the words to come from one single discourse: the sexual discourse. Had it been otherwise, I would regard my film as a failure. The chosen space certainly is that of love and death which, for me, covers the whole of Japan.

Q.: It would appear that you prevent us from regarding Sada as a murderess. The man, her victim, accepts and even invites his own destruction. Beyond the anecdotal level, you seem to be celebrating 'amour fou' as a religion of the Absolute.
A.: When applied to Sada, the word murderess shocks me, as it would astound any Japanese. At the start Sada and Kichi may appear to be mere libertines, but they move towards a kind of sanctification. I hope everybody will understand that.

Q.: *The Boy* and *Death by Hanging* refer to very recent events. *Empire of the Senses*, on the other hand, stems from something that happened forty years ago. What is its contemporary relevance to you?
A.: Events don't lose their actuality as long as they evoke an echo in us, regardless of whether they happened even in another century.

Q.: Some people will nevertheless reproach you for having abandoned your social and political concerns.
A.: Isn't it very significant to show one's indifference to politics?

Q.: What remains from the main theme of your previous films: childhood dreams – Japanese reality? Can this be found in the Oedipal relations which link these near-orphans Sada and Kichi to sexual partners older than themselves?
A.: I don't want to reject that kind of psychoanalytical approach, which you are free to use on my film. That is your responsibility. As far as I am concerned, I would ask: do young people know what to do with their lives? Later on, you begin to get an idea, and that is precisely what happens to my characters. They affirm their desires, in opposition to society.

Q.: Which are the key scenes for you?
A.: Each viewer has to answer that for him/herself.

Q.: To avoid misunderstandings, could you define for us what is understood by the terms geisha and prostitute in the Japan of 1936 and that of today?
A.: The term geisha comprises very different professional categories. It means 'to sell one's art', but on the bottom rungs of the social ladder it means 'to sell one's body'. In that context, let me add that according to notions specific to our country, the world of sensuality doesn't in the least detract from a person's value as a human being. That notion of *koshoku*, implying both 'capacity to appreciate' and 'knowing how to love', has never been neglected. In another era it even used to be a condition for being a gentleman. In the tenth century, *The Tale of Genji* founded aristocratic society in Japan, and for the first time in that society a sexual culture aspired towards a 'knowing how to love'. Polygamy and polyandry dominated in that aristocratic class. This refinement of erotic

Empire of the Senses

culture came to an end with the brutal era of the
samurai but re-emerged in the Edo Period from the
seventeenth to the nineteenth century. Of course,
that culture was the privilege of the dominant
classes who practised it in houses of pleasure. No
shame attached to those houses, absolutely not.
Monogamy was imposed in the Meiji Period, favouring
the economic modernisation of the country based on
an imported model. The beautiful tradition of
'knowing how to love' faded and died on the eve of
the Second World War. Sada and Kichi, my characters,
are the survivors of a sexual tradition that used
to exist and which to me is admirably Japanese.

Q.: The end of the film recalls that four days after
her crime, Sada was found resplendent with happiness
clutching her lover's attributes. Where does that
information come from?
A.: All the police reports say so and they provided
me with the inspiration for the final sequence;
without it my film would be false from start to
finish.

Q.: Your dialogues are short . . . pointillist.
Without trying to prove anything, you force us to
look, to feel, to think. That way, the film becomes
more personal, more intimate to each spectator.
A.: I preferred using short dialogues. Their
conciseness is well rendered by the French subtit-
les. Besides, the act of love doesn't need words.

Q.: 'Amour fou' seems to find its consummation in
the final castration. No doubt it would be wrong to
invoke the Christian notion of sin in that context?
A.: Yes, of course. And I don't want Kichi to evoke
the image of a crucified man.

Q.: Who forms part of your spiritual family?
A.: All those who wanted or want to change society
and all those who wanted or want to change
themselves. But if you ask me to choose between
people who are famous and those who aren't, I prefer
the company of those who aren't.

Q.: Of course, the Oshima aesthetic involves the
use of décor, costume, music. You always use the
same art director.
A.: In the beginning, I thought I was someone who
wanted to destroy all aesthetics and yet, film by

film, I discover an aesthetic of my own, especially since I met the eminent art director Jusho Toda. If I had to find an explanation, I would say that there is an interchange between a kind of asceticism and an ineffably Epicurean feeling. If I had to sum it up in one image, you would see a flame against a black or a very dark background. In that respect, *Empire of the Senses* deliberately shows the limits to which this aesthetic has led me.

Q.: Indeed, and this cannot but be deliberate, this is the first time that you have locked yourself into a physical and even a sexual action, fully aware of the misunderstandings that might arise.
A.: It's true, I felt completely free to make the film precisely how I wanted it to be.

Q.: In Japan, Sada is a popular figure. What does she represent and why did you dedicate a film to her?
A.: Sada's name is so popular in Japan that it suffices to pronounce it to touch on the most serious sexual taboos. It is quite natural that a Japanese artist should want to dedicate his work to that marvellous woman. Thanks to the magnificent collaboration of the actors and to the resources put at my disposal by the producers, I do not think I betrayed her image.

Q.: Do you obey any axiom, any rule?
A.: I have always dreamt of mixing dream and reality.

Q.: What is the subject of your next film?
A.: Ask M. Anatole Dauman.

Volker Schlöndorff   8000 Munich 22
                                      Obermaierstrasse 1

Dear Anatole,
    I have to tell you how enthusiastic I am about
Empire of Passion.
    Empire, imprison, prison – how often the second
film in a series is better than the preceding one,
and I hope that the title will attract many lovers
of real passion. They will find it here.
    By introducing the fantastic into a peasant drama,
adding Wilhelm Reich to Zola, Oshima rescues the
chronicle from the naturalism into which too many
meticulous reconstructions have drowned it.
    The authenticity and the savagery of the facts
could have made it into a story for Kurosawa. Oshima
filmed them with the quiet distance of an Ozu. To
this man and to this woman, brutalised by work,
poverty, ignorance, alcohol and idleness, he ac-
cords, without ever stressing the social aspects,
a pure passion that dreams only of 'living the life
of a "normal" couple for three days'. And those
lovers who can't unite for want of a voluptuous (or
just a human) space will die without ever having
reneged on their sensuality, as if that were the
ultimate identity of alienated people. Respecting
what others repress, they are treated like witches
in the Middle Ages. A tragedy treated like a
chronicle, with strange dialogue like in police
reports, with the usual characters of the formal
and beautiful lords, the vengeful mother, the madman
and the farcical policeman devoured by mosquitoes
who conducts a voyeuristic rather than a police
inquiry. Also medieval – at least for us Westerners
– is the flesh and blood presence of the corpse,
thirsting for alcohol and bleeding bright red blood.
    Others than me (perhaps Genêt) will find better
reasons for my enthusiasm. I congratulate you for
having the courage to make this Passion follow the
Senses.

Yours

Volker Schlöndorff

WIM WENDERS,
THE CREATURE OF THE CLOUDS

In 1952, Maurice Clavel took me to Königsberg, the land of imagination and philosophy, for a screen adaptation of Stendhal's novel, *Mina de Vanghel*. The writing of that novel, underpinned by the France-Germany couple, had so troubled the author and disturbed his method that he tried to write it all over again under the title *The Pink and the Green*.

Full of the passions of German Romanticism, the film was described by André Breton in these terms: 'Love catches fire in the wind it loves most, the wind of perdition.'

Having tried to show by means of cinematic light what cannot be spoken, together with Peter Schamoni and Max Ernst (*Exercice illégal de l'astronomie* and *Combien de couleurs dans la main?*), I started with Volker Schlöndorff on *Le Coup de grâce*, *Die Blechtrommel* and *Die Fälschung*, three films indifferent to the currents of fashion and driven towards metaphysical shores.

Then came Wim Wenders.

Paris, Texas tells of the wanderings of an amnesiac in the desert of his life; *Wings of Desire* is about a fallen angel falling in love and the giddiness of a trapezist. And *Until the End of the World* is about the act of seeing, deep within oneself, the images of the world surviving its dissolution. Wenders has made me share the fate of his heroes. He spared me nothing of his fertile and brilliant uncertainty. Between the happy end and the dead end, the Wunderkind has made me acquiesce in all the blows of fate.

I embarked on the Wendersian saga by way of my ex-wife, Pascale Dauman. She had started out as a brilliant first mate of the good ship Argos, then she became an instructress and finally she founded her own company, specialising in introducing into France top artists coming from the margins and to whom attaches a whiff of sulphur.

When a film is about to come out, everything depends on the way you can manage to astound people and on how fast you can go: you need a talent like hers, able to strike accurately and to practise a baroque seductiveness. And I bet that in this professional, seasoned by difficulties and associating with monsters, the audio-visual monopolies will find in the dark days they are promising us the Last of the Independents – last but not least. Her company, Pari Films,[1] has distinguished itself by co-financing two daring films by Wenders: *Nick's Movie* and especially *Der Stand der Dinge* [*The State of Things*]. The script of the latter film contains some noteworthy points that should be of great interest to the Creature of the Clouds' producers.

In a hotel badly damaged by a storm, on the Atlantic coast of Portugal, a film crew is waiting to do a remake of a classic science fiction film. They have run out of film stock and out of money. Gordon, the producer, has gone to Los Angeles with a few feet of the negative but has disappeared without trace. Passionately in love with cinema, perhaps even endowed with creative vision, he ventured way beyond what Hollywood understands by taking risks. Pursued by hit men, he has holed up in his trailer. This suits Fritz, the film's German director, who feels the need to pause and think about the film and to reflect on his entire career. A kind of madness besets the crew, their energies shot to pieces by the 'state of things'. They begin to doubt their own abilities and to fear the arrival of the money which would require them to go back into the limelight. All Fritz sees in the script is a vulgar and corrupting force obstructing his work.

He can't manage to think up broad structures, to think in terms of action. He is only interested in 'situations', especially real life ones rather than those of his film's 'story'. He waits for things to happen to his characters, but nothing does. That's the nub of the problem. Two mutually exclusive stories clash with each other: a love story and a death story. The director wants to make both, mixing comedy and horror. Gordon and Fritz know each other well and they will have to find a compromise. Soon they are together again in Los Angeles: 'What are we doing together?' Gordon asks, 'Me, a New Jersey Jew and you, a

Paris, Texas (*Harry Dean Stanton, Hunter Carson*)

Paris, Texas (*Nastassja Kinski*)

German director, the most boring guy I've ever known . . . Can you tell me what we are doing together?' The state of things draws to a close with a rare and touching event: like Dirty Harry pointing his Magnum, the director points his camera at the big scene, shooting the death of the producer as he is riddled by the bullets of his creditors . . . What fate did the camera of the Creature of the Clouds have in store for me? Film or death?

When making *Paris, Texas*, Wim went and shot the first act, set in Texas, before his German money had arrived. Coming to the second act, which starts off in Los Angeles when the amnesiac father meets his son, he ran out of money and the production stopped. Wim, as the executive producer, called me from deepest America to tell me that the technicians weren't being paid any more and that there was no money even to pay for daily living expenses. As far as I was concerned, I had fulfilled all my contractual obligations and I wasn't to be involved again until the post-production stage. In effect, my partner was asking to borrow money to stave off disaster. His voice on the phone sounded anxious: the Americans had gone back home but the Germans and the French were running out of food. No matter how often he went up and down Hollywood Boulevard, promises of money were few and uncertain, he insisted. I replied that I had followed the example of the producer he had caricatured in *Der Stand der Dinge* and had taken refuge in my trailer. Nevertheless, I gave in.

We came to the third act, where the father and son go looking for the mother who may be living in Houston. Wim was shooting twelve to fifteen hours a day with a perfectly cohesive crew. But this time, the film's life exhausted the script's resources. Wim was looking for an ending and some dialogues still had to be written. He roped in the child actor's father, a guy called 'Kit Carson'. At night, he tried to finish the script himself, using scraps of dialogue brought to him in small corner cafés, while consulting Sam Shepard by phone. The last scene was written on the eve of the final day of shooting. The script marathon had been won.

The last set: the peep show where he finds the mother, the love of his life, behind the one-way mirror. It was impossible to do any retakes of that twenty-seven minute sequence because Nastassja Kinski had to leave the next day to honour a previous engagement. Besides, they were down to their last metres of film stock. Everybody had to succeed, together, on the first take. They had to perform in unison a technical triple somersault without a net: Harry Dean Stanton, Nastassja Kinski, Robby Müller, Agnès Godard and Claire Denis, the flying trapezists of the peep show. The dangerous vault was accomplished to perfection.

The last act: the Cannes festival. Wim and his editor, Peter Przygodda, had been working night and day right to the last available second, while in Paris Bernard Eisenschitz was doing the French subtitled print at lightning speed. The festival had selected the film on the basis of a video that ran half an hour longer than the final version. D Day had been fixed as late in the schedule as possible, three days from the end of the competition. The print arrived in Cannes by courier the day before the screening. Nastassja Kinski, pregnant, arrived on the day itself, half an hour after the press conference had started. But fortune smiled upon us. The festival audience, often cold and aloof, didn't spare its warm applause. Thus ended the odyssey of *Paris, Texas*.

For many years, Wim carried within him the idea of a science fiction film inspired by his first encounter with the Australian outback: the red earth from where you can watch the rest of the world, externalising the images you have within yourself. Before finding refuge amongst the Australian Aborigines, the heroes of *Until the End of the World* travel all over the world collecting the most important 'sights' to safeguard them and store them in dreams that will then be passed on to the blind survivors in the after-world. Once liberated from *Paris, Texas*, Wim went from one capital city to another gathering an impressive amount of documentation. After a year and a half, he had devised a structure: it took him four hours just to narrate the film to me. The film itself seemed to be about five or six hours long and would require an astronomical budget. In short, an impossible film, forcing Road Movies, his own production company, as well as myself to admit defeat. Having founded the co-operative Filmverlag der Autoren, Wim feels compelled to produce his own films: his art cannot bear the constraints imposed by authority, only those dictated by inspiration. His sole Hollywood experience, *Hammett*, turned out to be a failure whereas all his other films are triumphs of self-management. Alongside the Creature of the Clouds, the role of co-producer is simply that of directing conscience.

But for *Until the End of the World*, Wim felt on his producer's brow the touch of cold steel wielded by the great artist intent on self-fulfilment. He gave up trying to impose on himself the terrible test of vampirising his own producer's blood. Nevertheless, the desire to shoot tormented him every bit as much as the irresistible wish to renew his *mise en scène*. In a sense, he had broken with America, his adoptive country, and awaiting the moment when he would embark on his next migration, he was suddenly struck by the fact that he was German and he saw the gleam of a film devoted to the city of Berlin. One day, he came to see me to talk about his desire for an 'indescribable film'. Ten minutes of explanation were enough to sweep away the depressing memory of five hours of *Until the End of the World*. He read me a poem by Rilke which had first shown him the way into the film:

> At night I want to talk to the angel
> To find out if he recognises my eyes
> If he suddenly asked me: are you looking at Eden?
> I would have to answer: Eden is burning.
>
> I want to lift my mouth towards him
> Hard as one who has no desire
> And the angel would say: are you aware of life?
> And I would have to say: Life is gnawing away.
>
> And if he found this joy in me
> Which in his mind becomes eternal
> And if he raised it in his hands
> I would have to say: joy has gone astray.

(Extract from a poem for Lou Albert-Lasard by Rainer Maria Rilke)

The heroes would be angels observing the life of the Berliners, so different from that of other Germans because so close to the presence of that which makes one German. No other city is to the same degree 'the historical site of truth', the domain of invisible figures from the past and from the future, the symbol of survival. Wim wanted to see Berlin from the sky, through the eyes of angels, in order to talk about that perennial question: how to live? And the unthinkable would happen: the angels would be attracted by the human condition and one of them would fall in love so deeply that he becomes mortal.

After that story, the desire to co-produce was almost instantaneous for both of us. There was no need to spend time worrying about technical or artistic matters. The angels would take care of that. But everything seemed to conspire to force us to shoot at the least favourable time: the last months of 1986. Would the angels be able to prevent the winter snows? They were. For the first time in decades, it didn't snow in Berlin until the very end of the year. The miracle of this co-production made in heaven launched *Wings of Desire*, a German film about the specificity of being German, adorned by the poetry of Rainer Maria

Rilke and by the texts of Peter Handke, to a worldwide success crowned in the land of the rising sun: 200,000 tickets in a few months in one single Tokyo cinema. The distributor, my friend Hayao Shibata, the 'speed god', paid tribute to the achievement in the following terms: 'Congratulations to you, to Wim, to all of you for an unbroken 300-day first run in Tokyo for your miraculous masterpiece. I asked what something should be called when it goes beyond the miraculous, but Wim hasn't replied yet. Silence. Perhaps, for it to continue . . . ?'

From the ruined hotel on the Atlantic coast where *The Survivors* couldn't be made to *Wings of Desire* and the desire for a film saved from the snow, the state of things in world cinema has turned into a state of grace for the career of the Creature of the Clouds.

At the centre of the Wendersian creation always remains a fascination for 'the act of seeing'. To see objectively and subjectively. To see from the sky, to see in dreams, to see inside oneself. To see by way of the camera, of a computer, through another person by proxy. What will be the future of seeing? 'You can't change the world, but you can still change the images of the world,' Wenders said to the Cannes audience when he received the best director's prize for *Wings of Desire* in 1987.

We set off together to the end of the world, to Australia, for the wanderer's last film. To the bureaucrats of the Australian Film Commission, who wanted to force him to sacrifice Robby Müller, his cameraman, or Peter Przygodda, his editor, his companions for twenty years on nearly all his films, the Creature of the Clouds replied superbly: 'You will cut off neither my right nor my left hand.'

At 45 degrees in the shade, in the most absolute deserts of the world, thinking about his astronomical budget, will the producer of *Mina de Vanghel* at last settle accounts with his Germanicness and will he too be captured by the camera and saved from perdition to figure in the last images of the Wendersian world?

NOTE

1. Pari Films was founded by Pascale Dauman in 1973. The first films it distributed were: Ruy Guerra's *The Gods and the Dead* and *Pink Narcissus*. Pascale Dauman also put together programming packages around themes (e.g. Experimental American Cinema) or authors (e.g. Emile De Antonio, Frederick Wiseman, Jean Rouch).

Pari Films will introduce to the French public a number of films by Ozu, Josef von Sternberg's *Saga of Anatahan* and Ichikawa's *Yukinojo Henge*. Over the last few years, Pascale Dauman has distributed films by Jim McBride, Michael Radford, Jean-François Stévenin, Peter Greenaway, Stephen Frears, Raymond Depardon, Wim Wenders, Jim Jarmusch, Terence Davies and Mike Leigh.

Argos Films
4 rue Édouard-Nortier
92200 Neuilly-sur-Seine

Neuilly, 21 October 1986

M. Charles VANEL
MOUANS SARTOUX 06

Re.: *Wings of Desire*

Dear Sir,

My friend Wim Wenders thought that you might agree to do him the great honour of appearing as yourself in his next film, which he has just started shooting in Berlin, by way of a tribute to the great era of world cinema which you exemplify so gloriously.

I was delighted by this suggestion although worried that the constraints of the script and of the shooting schedule might end up frustrating the director's enthusiasm and reduce excessively the interest of the part proposed to you.

The fear of being unable to offer you a part worthy of you unfortunately has been confirmed and the painful duty has fallen to me of informing you that Wim Wenders needed to eliminate some ambitious developments from his work, forcing him to forgo the tribute he planned to pay to you personally.

Our sadness at not being able to meet you on the thrilling adventure Wim Wenders is preparing for us in Berlin is increased by our embarrassment at having caused you considerable inconvenience by submitting the proposition to you in the first place.

On my behalf, as well as on behalf of Wim Wenders and of all his collaborators, I would like to express our regret and to assure you of the affectionate admiration which, although it now cannot be expressed in the film, nevertheless will remain warmly alive in each of us as we remember your immense career.

Wim Wenders asked me to tell you that he would very much like to come and see you and talk to you about his projects on his next visit to France if you would be so kind as to overlook the abandonment of this project and to accord him the pleasure of meeting with you.

Most sincerely,

Anatole DAUMAN

Argos Films
4, rue Édouard-Nortier
92200 Neuilly-sur-Seine

Neuilly, 6 November 1986

Mr Wim Wenders
Road Movies
Potsdamerstrasse 199
1000 Berlin 30

Dear Friend,
   Your reassuring news leads me to believe that 'The sky over Berlin' will soon have yielded its mysteries and that your creative spirit will resume its journey barely interrupted by the encounter with the Angels. I therefore have the duty to devote my spare time to the task of getting a little closer to the horizon of your next film.
   Allow me for a moment to direct your attention to *Until the End of the World* and to ask you to sign the enclosed statement concerning the cession of your copyright to ROAD MOVIES and to ARGOS FILMS. This formality, which you already completed for *Paris, Texas*, is required to register the film with the Public Register of Cinematography in France. Of course, this is just a modest beginning for this future co-production.

In friendship,

Anatole Dauman

PREVIEW DESCRIPTION OF AN INDESCRIBABLE FILM

Text by Wim Wenders about *Wings of Desire*

Shall I attempt to describe something when, at the outset, all I can write is this: *a desire, desires*?

Whoever wants to make a film, write a book, paint a picture, in short wants to invent something, begins with that, with a desire.

You desire that something exist. You work at it. You want to add something to the world, something more beautiful, something truer; or simply, to create something other than what exists already.

Oh, the beginning! As soon as desire is aroused, you already imagine something other than what is there; already the light of something else shines through. So you have to head towards the light, hoping to remain true to the original desire.

For a film, alas, you have to start by accounting for your desire. Even more troublesome, you have to describe in advance the road to be travelled.

I desired, I saw the light beginning to gleam of a film *in* and *about* Berlin.

A film that would include a certain idea of this city as it has been since the end of the war. A film that would at last show what has always been missing in all films shot in Berlin even though it seems so obvious: feelings, of course, but also that something in the air, under your feet, which so radically distinguishes life here from life elsewhere, in other cities.

Let me come back to my desire for this film. I want to add that it is the desire of someone who has long been absent from Germany and who never could nor would recognise anywhere other than in this city *what it is that makes you German*. And yet, I am not a Berliner. For the past twenty years, my visits here were for me my only truly *German experiences*, because here history is physically and emotionally present, a history which cannot be lived elsewhere in Germany – in the Federal Republic – except as disavowal or as absence.

Of course, I desired even more that this film speak, here, of the only undying question: *How to live?*

So, *Berlin* represents also, in that desire, the world, because it is 'a historical site of truth'.[1] *No other city is to such an extent a symbol, to such an extent a site of survival.*

Berlin is as divided as our world, our epoch, as each of our experiences. Many say that Berlin is 'screwed'. I say: Berlin is more real than any other city. It is a site rather than a city.

. . . To live in this city of undivided truth, associating with the invisible figures of the future and of the past . . . That's my desire, on the way to a film.

My story doesn't talk about Berlin merely because it happens to be set there, but because it could not happen anywhere else.

NOTE

1. From the programme of the exhibition 'Mythos Berlin, Concept'.

Filming Wings of Desi

BUDGET FOR *WINGS OF DESIRE*

FEATURE FILM
Wings of Desire

produced by

Argos Films (France) and Road Movies (Germany)

Final budget established by the Executive Producer
(Road Movies)

On 30 September 1987

	Deutschmarks	French Francs
I SCRIPT		
Subject, adaptation, dialogues	45,000	145,350
Director's copyright	48,121.95	155,433.89
Music rights and extra script costs	98,173.40	317,100.08
II PERSONNEL		
Director	115,000	371,450
Executive Producer	115,800	374,034
Technicians: Camera Crew	804,034.65	2,597,031.91
Technicians: Set Construction and Decoration	171,128.12	552,743.76
Craftsmen: Camera Crew	161,730.93	522,390.90
Craftsmen: Set Construction and Decoration	48,302.22	156,016.17
III CAST		
Principal Parts	448,239.62	1,447,813.97
Supporting Parts	90,804.61	293,298.89
Small Parts, extras, doubles, etc.	116,725.56	377,023.55
IV SOCIAL CHARGES ON SALARIES	314,330.30	1,015,286.86
V STUDIOS	49,933.99	161,286.78
VI LOCATIONS – EXTERIORS		
General expenditure	92,029.83	297,256.35
Lighting	145,403.68	469,653.88
Travel and subsistence	412,627.23	1,332,782.95
VII SUPPLIES		
Camera and sound	228,103.51	930,574.33
Sets, Special Effects, Furniture	509,922.30	1,647,049.05
Equipment, Transport	84,489.22	272,900.18
Editing, Dubbing, Mix	160,350.14	517,930.95

```
VIII FILMSTOCK
     Filmstock                        130,083.14     420,168.54
     Laboratory                       423,989.37   1,369,488.80

IX MISCELLANEOUS
     Insurance                        118,784.10     383,672.64
     Management and miscellaneous
     costs (except general overheads) 195,844.52     632,577.79

Cost before overheads              5,188,952.39  16,760,316.22


     Overheads                        226,237.83     730,748.19

Cost before tax                    5,415,190.22  17,491,064.41
```

11 November
1987

Agreed	True and fair to the best of our knowledge and belief
The French Co-producer The Président-Directeur Général	The Executive Producer
Argos Films S.A.	*Road Movies Gmbh*

Wim Wenders with the bunches of garlic Anatole Dauman sent him on 15 October 1986, for the first day of shooting on Wings of Desire. *The accompanying telegram read: 'Garlic, lots of garlic. That is the most precious encouragement I could possibly give you for this first day of shooting.'*

PRODUCTION COMPANY:

DAILY PROGRESS REPORT N°. 50

TITLE: "DER HIMMEL ÜBER BERLIN"	DIRECTOR: WIM WENDERS	DATE: 10.2.198

STARTED 20.10.1986	FINISHING DATE 14.2.1987	SCENE NUMBERS

		LOCATION OF WORK/SET		
ESTIMATED DAYS	40	Esplanade	COMPLETED 520	
DAYS TO DATE	50	Bellevuestr. 16-18A		
REMAINING DAYS	3	1000 Berlin 21	PART	
DAYS OVER	14			
UNDER				

TIME			SCRIPT SCENES					
				SCRIPT		EXTRA		RETAK
CALL	12.00		NUMBER	MINUTES	NUMBER	MINUTES	NUMBER	MIN
1st SET UP COMPLETED	16.15							
LUNCH FROM	13.25	PREVIOUSLY TAKEN		105'15"				
TO	13.55	TAKEN TO-DAY		7'30"				
UNIT DISMISSED	0.30	TAKEN TO DATE		112'45"				
		TO BE TAKEN +		12'45"	DAILY AVERAGES OVERALL:2'			
TOTAL HOURS	12,5							
Dinner break 19.00-19.20		TOTAL SCRIPT SCENES		–	STUDIO:		LOCATION:	

ACTION PROPS AND EFFECTS		SLATE NUMBERS		STILLS		
1 mixing board		308		B & W		COLOUR
concert equipment	via PA Excellemt	PREVIOUSLY TAKEN	PREVIOUSLY TAKEN		164	
		8	TAKEN TO-DAY		–	
		SET UPS: 316	TAKEN TO DATE		164	

CONTRACT ARTISTES								CROWDS	
NAME	W	S/B	RE	CALL	ARR	D'SS'D			RATE
Bruno Ganz	33/1			14.00	15.15	21.00	117 Extras		50,–
Otto Sander	25/2			14.00	15.15	0.30	2 Bits		100.–
Solveig Dommartin	17/1			13.00	15.15	23.00	7 Bits		80,–
Nick Cave	1			11.00		0.30			
Bad Seeds	1			11.00		0.30			

ADDITONAL CREWS

2 Beleuchter
Concerttechniker
3 Helfer
Peter Arnold } 2nd camera
Martin Kukula }
Ingrid Bendzuk (2. Maske)

PICTURE				FILM FOOTAGES		SOUND	
sch/w	colour	s/w 2nd	colour 2nd		TOTAL	½" TAPE	
44.236	6.943	8.550	–	PREVIOUSLY USED		135	
642	1.960	110	910	USED TO-DAY		10	
44.878	8.903	8.660	910	TOTALS TO DATE		145	

SHORT ENDS:		WASTE:	

REMARKS: Beleuchtungs- und Bühnencrew Arbeitsbeginn 11.00.
Beleuchtungs u. Kameraequipment via Intervision
Tonequipment via A. Arft
Produktionsfahrzeuge via Bär.
Catering via Bovril 40 Personen + 150 Dinner.

Call sheet for Wings of Desire

THE ACT OF SEEING

(About some futuristic aspects of Wim Wenders' film
Until the End of the World.)

Situated between 1998 and 2003, this film should be
shot in seventeen countries, and especially in
Europe, Japan, the United States and in Australia.
In a near future, our way of life should have evolved
in certain ways: for instance, there would be public
or private videophones, extra-flat high definition
television monitors for aircraft passengers, word-
processing machines and micro-computers, various
audio and video gadgets, etc. The film will reflect
this anticipated evolution but its real interest,
its main driving force or, if you like, its futurist
message concerns the evolution of *vision*. The actual
subject of the film is *the act of seeing*, consciously
as well as unconsciously, in its oneiric dimension,
through dreams. (These aspects will be developed in
the scenario and in the visuals on the screen.)
   In our film, thanks to state of the art information
technology, a blind man would at last have access
to vision, someone who cannot see would be able to
see, and what's more, thanks to electronic imagery
he would be able to see 'through the eyes' of someone
who is able to see. How would this be possible? In
Germany, various doctors and scientists were consulted about such an eventuality and they didn't
judge it to be an unlikely proposition (although
definitely a futurist one). Some found it an
interesting notion, even a plausible one.
   The plot summary would go something like this:
Around 1998, computers exist that are able to 'see'.
Having been fed incessantly for years with detailed
and constantly updated information, these computers
have learned to distinguish colours, silhouettes
and forms. They can also decipher the meanings of
those things. So they are able to differentiate
between one object and another, to tell a dog from
a cat and one man from another. That is the basic
idea we start from.
   This idea implies, amongst other things, the
existence of a cameraman, that is to say, of someone
who 'takes' images: a 'seer' who lends his eyes to
those who do not see. The one who sees does so, in
a way, in the place of the one who cannot see thanks
to video-glasses with lenses designed to register

Wim Wenders,
location-scouting in
Australia for Until the
End of the World

on tape precise and perfectly defined images. The
'objective image' thus obtained – let's call it that
for clarity's sake – goes together with a stereo
sound-track (double track: original sound and
ambient noise track) recorded at the same time in
perfect synchrony. That is the least futurist aspect
of the story.

While this video camera records precisely the
images captured by the 'image taker' with his video
glasses, another machine records at the same time
the telepathic waves emitted by his brain while he
is in the act of seeing. Infinitely more sophisticated and more accurate than the various machines
currently used, for instance, to make encephalo-
grams, this ultra-sensitive apparatus can even
record plasmatic waves and represent them in the
form of an image, here called 'a subjective image'.

Then both the subjective and the objective images
are fed into a computer. In other words, both what
the cameraman sees and what goes through his mind
in that very same moment will be put into the
computer. That represents a huge quantity of
simultaneous information. The computer can decipher
the objective image all by itself. But what happens
to the subjective image, necessarily connected with
the objective one? Proceeding by way of comparisons,
two computers should be able to decipher the
information provided by the brain and, through a
mind-bogglingly complex tangle of millions of
encephalographic data, should be able to understand
how exactly the cameraman saw things and to what
degree his cerebral activity corresponds to the real
images. So the computer tries to work out its own
programme learning to imitate the brain, which is
a difficult operation for a mere machine. The data
of the subjective image could be too complex, too
incoherent, too difficult to decipher and to process
to allow the computer to understand how the brain,
after various electrical and biochemical processes,
arrives at an image.

The cameraman who personally saw and recorded how
he saw what he saw, has to re-view the views he
took. Sitting in a darkened room in front of a high
definition screen, he needs total concentration in
order to be able to re-view the images he had seen
with his own eyes, 'live'. The waves emitted by his
brain will also be recorded and fed into the
computer. Then the computer will dispose of enough
images to understand or evaluate to what extent the

subjective image (consisting of brain waves) corresponds to the objective images which it visualises at the same time, of course. So the computer will be able to compare the rudimentary primary data provided by the brain, corresponding to the *act of seeing*, to the processed data corresponding to the *act of understanding*. While re-viewing these same images, which it knows to be objective images, the computer will be able to combine the two types of data, to add one to the other and then to determine, through some filtering process, to which specific cerebral processes correspond particular aspects of image production. It will understand how the human brain was able to see and it will be able to identify the vision of a given image, to reconstitute that information in the form of complex data, the specific frequencies of the cerebral activities able to produce the image in question. The computer will be able to reproduce the very image seen by the cameraman and to translate it for the use of those who cannot see by triggering in the non-sighted person's brain the specific frequencies of the cerebral waves involved. Obviously, the non-sighted person will be able to listen first to the transmission of the sound-image that goes with the visual experience of what he is supposed to register. That is the point at which a non-sighted person will be able to see; a blind person will be able to see, while remaining dependent on the intensity of the way the cameraman has 'taken' the views, on the quality of his own reinterpretation of those same scenes, on the accuracy with which the computer will have evaluated the interference between the two moments of vision (the initial vision and the re-viewing) and, finally, on the value of the comparison the computer was able to make between those data and the real image. In the mind of the non-sighted, images will appear, perhaps often rather unfocused ones, or fogged ones, reduced to mere shadows or vague silhouettes, but perhaps at times also perfectly clear ones, perfectly recognisable ones, if only in momentary flashes.

Of course, nobody will ever know what the blind person actually sees. The people involved in the experiment can only see an objective image, on the high-definition screen. Nevertheless, in the lab there may perhaps be another giant screen showing simulations of the computer's interpretation of the information received and sent to the blind person's brain: unclear images, dim ones, fogged ones, out of which suddenly some detail would emerge, or a clear image.

Anyway, from such a premise one would clearly be able to derive incredible images – quite literally, things that have never been seen. Especially if, as will be the case in this story, this invention has been diverted, inverted or perverted and the computer learns to decode oneiric images, and to project, onto a giant screen, dream images which perhaps nobody was ever meant to see. In this respect too, the script would have to be more explicit. But the synopsis already gives some idea of the possibilities offered by this invention.

Wim Wenders, September 1988

ENCLOSURES

WALERIAN BOROWCZYK

Jean Paul Sarré and Anatole Dauman interview
Walerian Borowczyk.

JPS & AD: You choose to be the author of films which
all manifest identical preoccupations even though
they may be set in different epochs and form part
of a wide variety of genres, ranging from the popular
serial to the adaptation of classic novels: *Blanche*
was based on *Mazepa* by Juliusz Slowacki, *La Marée*
was based on André Pieyre de Mandiargues and soon
you will start *La Marge*. In the case of *La Bête*,
you wrote an original script that raises many
questions. You place in a contemporary setting the
loves between man and beast celebrated so often in
antiquity and the artistic representations of which
can be admired in museums the world over. It still
remained for the cinema to provide a new image of
it. Did you want to evoke the memory of the Centaurs,
those legendary beings half-man half-beast who
notoriously disrupted King Pirithous' wedding?
WB: Our minds are populated by legendary figures,
we remember things we have read and various artistic
representations in which animals or hybrid monsters
appear. But in my film, it isn't just a matter of
evoking that. *La Bête* is a fantasy film and
especially an 'adult film'. But first of all it is
a film about dream mechanisms. Dreams translate our
deepest desires. Why then cover with a veil of
silence the temptation of an intimate relationship
with an animal? The origins of the human body are
well known, and the copulation with a siren can thus
represent a sublime joy thanks to the medium of
dreams. Of course, *La Bête* is set in a less distant
era and the chosen animal is by no means a fish.

JPS & AD: In order to avail yourself of external

Walerian Borowczyk's La Bête

support, do you separate out the various stages of
film-making: writing the script, editing, etc.?
WB: All stages of a film's creation are in me at
one and the same time. My temperament does not allow
me to create only part of a work and then to entrust
the rest to specialists. Cinema is not a synthetic
art. People confuse cinema with the film industry.
Cinema certainly does need experienced specialists,
as does painting, which cannot exist without paint
manufacturers, makers of brushes and of linen
canvases.

JPS & AD: People have been able to admire the
extraordinary fascination exerted by the images in
all your films, and yet you do not use the same
directors of photography every time. In what special
way do you manage to elicit from your diverse
collaborators such superior expressive work?
WB: Like everyone else, you called them 'directors
of photography'. What a monstrous nomenclature! Why
not CEO [Chief Executive Officer] of photography!
I look through the camera's viewfinder and I
eliminate things. *That's the secret.* I also eliminate the collaborators who dare to try and barter
my own ideas with me. *I know everything.* And that
very often drives members of my crew to tears.

JPS & AD: The way you compose your shots betrays
your taste for painting. Which painters do you feel
closest to?
WB: I feel particularly close to nature and to
dreams, the two elements which make up 'imagination'. Every epoch has given me a few of my
favourite painters, often not so well known ones,
artists I discover. Since my childhood I have
remained impressed by the paintings of my father,
also by Tomasso Capelli, an Italian painter of the
fourteenth century, and by Henri Lecourbe.

JPS & AD: At a time when many insect species are
diminishing because of insecticides and various
aspects of pollution, what does *La Bête* mean to you?
Haven't you created an individual who defies the
laws of genetics and obeys those of belief and
malediction?
WB: You attribute to me the power of reacting quickly
to modern events which require us to take a position.
The disappearance of swallows because of insecticides I find very disturbing. We must create

eternal animals. *La Bête* may be regarded as a disavowal of death. It replaces the unfortunate swallows. It belongs to a more resistant type of fauna and answers to more than one vocation.

JPS & AD: Don't you perhaps want to be a creator of beings, and it may be that one of your motifs is the exploration of the double through a recourse to all the resources of the Fantasy genre? Do you expect the Fantasy genre to suggest a solution to the anxiety generated by the body?
WB: I expect little. I realise things. Women walking their little dogs on empty pavements in the morning, they envisage solutions to the problem of the body. It is hard to verify how many of them find those solutions . . . in the evening. The beast created in my film is in everybody's reach.

JPS & AD: You have made films with the greatest actors: Pierre Brasseur, Michel Simon, now the legendary Marcel Dalio. Have you had to pay a price for such a collaboration?
WB: Orators and bad actors 'act' in life. Great actors live on the stage. That's called sincerity. The unforgettable moment is when their lives are fixed onto celluloid. And it is they who are the best witnesses to their epoch.

JPS & AD: Your previous film, *Histoire d'un péché*, was selected for the 28th Cannes Festival, where it marked and divided opinion. For some it was a popular melodrama, for others an accomplished baroque work. Some saw in it the mark of genius. Whether you are on the banks of the Vistula or on those of the Seine, don't you above all seize the opportunity to allow the forces of dream to act within you?
WB: Of course, I remain faithful to myself and faithfulness knows no boundaries. The opinions and the verdicts pronounced bear witness more to the quality of those who pronounce them than to that of a work.

JPS & AD: Would you have liked to live with another identity in some other epoch?
WB: If I were to find myself in the body of a knight or of a monk in the Middle Ages it wouldn't stop my brain from thinking and wouldn't alter my worries. But if I have to choose an epoch and an identity, it would be that of Leda's swan in antiquity (if

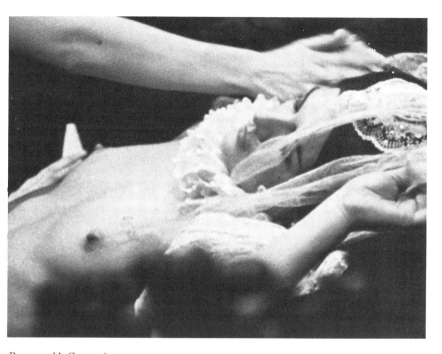

Borowczyk's Contes immoraux

she really was as beautiful as the artists represent her).

JPS & AD: In *La Bête*, do you, this time elevating it to the dimension of myth, continue and extend the detailed and passionate study of pleasure which already led you to make *Une collection particulière* and *Contes immoraux*?

WB: *La Bête* isn't the third part of a triptych but I like your expression 'a detailed and passionate study' because I attach a great deal of importance to details.

Gabrielle Lazure in La Belle Capt

ALAIN ROBBE-GRILLET

'The Fiancée of Corinth'
Interview with Alain Robbe-Grillet about *La Belle Captive*

Q: Like your most recent novel, *Djinn*, this *Belle Captive* seems decidedly more accessible to the wider public than your previous films. Has your approach changed?
Alain Robbe-Grillet: If it's more accessible, all the better! But to me it certainly isn't a question of giving in to tastes other than my own. Simply: the images and the sounds I had in my mind on this occasion probably fit more easily into the frame of 'tellable story', and I know that is important for the public.

Q: Could you tell that story?
ARG: Yes, of course! But I'd prefer to tell it in a number of different ways; there are three or four possible stories – maybe more – in play in the bizarre adventure of the hero.

Q: You could start by telling us one of them.
ARG: That would be first of all the Greek legend of 'the fiancée of Corinth', whose recurrent trace has reached us particularly through an *Elegy* of Goethe's and a chapter of Michelet's *La Sorcière*. This is it: a young man falls in love with a blonde and pale young woman who attracts him irresistibly while remaining distant, enigmatic, evasive. She demands that he go and ask her parents in Corinth for her hand. He arrives there at dusk after a long journey. When the father and the mother understand the purpose of his visit, they appear terrified: their only daughter, they say, has been dead for seven years. They nevertheless offer the traveller shelter for the night. The only free room is, of course, that of the departed one who, wearing a white translucent dress, comes and lies next to the sleeping young man, whose blood she sucks until he is dead.

Q: Do you believe in ghosts?
ARG: No, not really, like everyone else, no doubt. But I grew up in their company. In the old house in Brest, surrounded by storm-tossed trees that at night would add their moans to sound of the foghorns

warning lost ships against reefs, I would be told
bedtime stories of ghosts, the wandering souls of
drowned sailors who formed the bulk of Breton
folklore. After that, I would toss and turn in my
sleep, dreaming bloody nightmares which soon con-
taminated my adolescent erotic dreams . . . If it
is true that the stories wrought by novelists and
film-makers come from their childhood, you would no
doubt have to look for an important part of my
inspiration in the Breton legends, or that would at
least be one of the possible keys.

Q: Now give us another key to your film.
ARG: Well, it could also be the classic story of
the 'thwarted mission'. A man has been charged with
a mission, a very important mission, but he doesn't
know precisely what he's supposed to do or the exact
purpose of the mission. An unforeseen event diverts
him from its accomplishment – temporarily, he
thinks. Here, this takes the form of a pretty girl
lying unconscious on the road at night and the hero
at the wheel of his car almost runs her over. In
helping the wounded woman he finds himself embroiled
in a series of adventures which (he thinks) don't
concern him, and he tries to get out of them. Too
late he will understand that, in fact, that was the
very mission with which he had been entrusted.

Q: But why that title, *La Belle Captive*, the
beautiful captive?
ARG: This inanimate girl placed in his way, in the
middle of the road, on a bend, with blood on her
thighs and a ripped dress, also has her hands tied
together behind her. She is like the still living
bait on the hook. As for the fiancée of Corinth,
she is what is called a captive soul. Because she
was murdered she can't find rest in a grave: she is
the prisoner of a crime, and it is in order to free
herself from this curse that she must drink the
blood of the living, in the hope of eventually
drinking the life of her killer. And then, the
beautiful captive could also be our fantasmatic
imaginary . . .

Q: It is also a famous painting by Magritte?
ARG: Of course. Magritte even painted five or six
canvases with that same title. With the permission
of his widow, I imagined a seventh variant in which
you can find the essential elements of the original:

red theatre drapes, slightly open, on a deserted beach, with in the background the sea and the breaking waves. In the foreground, in front of the curtain, there is a painter's easel with a tableau reproducing the sand and the waves and the horizon in the exact place where they are in the landscape, as if you saw them through red velvet. I think that's one of the 'fantastic' genre's favourite themes.

Q: Is that a possible third story of your *Belle Captive*?

ARG: Yes, if you want: beyond the visible world, there is another one which resembles ours exactly but which is 'false', and all our actions have their counterpart in that world . . . Or else, on the contrary, our world is the false one . . . That's also the way our dreams work. They are lies, if you like, but in a way they are truer than waking life, of which they are the double, or the inverse. In my film, the components of that fake Magritte appear on the screen every time the fiancée's teeth enter the flesh of her victim, in the nape of the neck, as if the vampire's bite immediately triggered the recurrent dream of immense theatre curtains opening out onto the sea. And as the hero becomes weaker, he goes deeper into that after-world without knowing that it is only a staging of his own death.

Q: So it is a vampire film?

ARG: It is at any rate a film that plays with some of the essential signs of that genre, and of the fantasy genre in general: parallel worlds that suddenly communicate via hidden spaces, the dead returning to grab the living, extremely pretty women thirsting for blood, dreams coming true, mad doctors experimenting with machines that inscribe dreams into the brain, etc.

Q: A second young woman, a brunette this time, occupies at least as important a place on the screen as the mysterious fiancée. Who is she?

ARG: Yes, the splendid amazon dressed in black leather astride a gleaming motorbike. She is the boss of the organisation which gave the hero his initial mission. And, in a parallel world, you discover that in fact she is also his wife. At the start she appears as a kind of guardian angel protecting the man from his temptations and weak-nesses: she tries to get him away from the

sweet-faced blonde vampire. But in the end the image
is inverted because stereotypes always are two-
sided . . .

Q: You often talk of stereotypes and you like using
the coded, even over-coded signs of the common
fantasy repertoire. Does that mean that it is an
abstract game for you which doesn't really involve
you personally?

ARG: Well no, on the contrary! Even when they are
part of an established repertoire and regardless of
the obviousness of their cultural or analytical
meaning, to us the ghosts of our dreams appear to
be very 'real'. It is their presence that strikes
us far more than their symbolism. The same goes for
my narratives (novels and films): those characters
emerging from the night in *La Belle Captive*, those
decors gradually breaking into shreds, those events
disconnecting from each other or turning back upon
themselves, to me they are true. I believe in them
absolutely, I hear them, I see them in my head,
otherwise I would not be able to narrate them. I
live with them, for a few months, a few years, as
I used to live with the spectres of my childhood.

Q: The images of this film look quite different from
those of your previous work. Did you have a good
understanding with Henri Alekan?

ARG: A wonderful one. Obviously, I didn't turn to
him just to reproduce the lacquered, flat image
without optical depth that I had wanted for
Glissements progressifs du plaisir or for *L'Eden et
après*. This time I needed very calculated lighting
effects, very directional ones, as in the theatre
where light is used to create bright spots that
isolate a few discontinuous fragments against a
dimly lit background. I needed fog, uncertainty,
apparitions suddenly springing from the shadows. It
was also necessary to mark very strongly the contrast
between the scenes that comprised the flow of the
narration (in an ill-defined and rather nocturnal
suburban area) and the holes suddenly punched into
that space by the violent light of fantasy: the
immense shore with the red drapes flapping in the
wind. We shot everything on location, but we
constantly had to transform the natural decor
through some more or less noticeable artifice.
Alekan revelled in it: he put so much enthusiasm
and vivacity into his work that at times it was

difficult to resist him when he suggested an orange sea or mauve faces!

Q: You also did a few shots on video?
ARG: Yes, a few minutes. Magritte's painting, in its overall composition, seems to prefigure the video technique called 'inset': holes in the landscape through which you discover parallel worlds. Hence the idea of using that effect for what Lewis Carroll calls going through the mirror. The action (or the feeling) of 'going through', of 'penetrating', plays a big role in the film. However, I haven't overused video effects because, in its current stage of development, the magnetic image lacks finesse and its manipulation remains hazardous and imprecise.

Alain Robbe-Grillet and Anatole Dauman at a première in Martinique

ELIA KAZAN

Beyond the Aegean
By Elia Kazan

Synopsis

Anatolia, 1919. With the blessing of the Allied
powers, a Greek armada lands at the port of Smyrna
to reclaim a territory which all Greeks believe
theirs by historical right. To the politicians of
Athens, this expedition is a holy crusade; to the
Greek minority of Anatolia a long-awaited liberation; to the Western nations which covet the oil
wealth of the Middle East, a mere episode in the
treacherous intrigues of the post-war years.

During this invasion, in the dead of night, a
sailboat disembarks two passengers on a rugged shore
near Smyrna: STAVROS, a strong, wiry 40-year-old,
and his younger brother, MICHAELIS, who has recently
lost an arm in the struggle against the Turks. Over
the past twenty years, Stavros, the hero of *The
Anatolian Smile* (US title: *America, America*), has
pulled himself up from abject poverty. Embracing
capitalism as his religion and propelled by relent-
less ambition, he has attached himself to Mr FERNAND,
a wealthy and cynical Armenian rug merchant,
eventually becoming his associate.

While the Greek population of Smyrna is busy
celebrating their army's victory, the two brothers
set out to perform a sacred duty. They seek out the
port official who embezzled money sent by Stavros
to pay for his family's journey to America. The
official, claiming that the hard-earned dollars were
used to bribe the Turkish authorities, had slowly
tortured the father with false hopes, humiliating
him for years and finally causing his death.
Michaelis takes it upon himself to execute the
exploiter.

Convinced that commerce is 'the only form of war
that counts', Stavros sees the defeated Turkish
majority of Anatolia as an untapped reservoir of
cheap labour. He proceeds to win the loyalty of
destitute local weavers, by supplying them with
looms, wool, dyes and even advances in cash. His
ambition is to establish 'a new America', a land of
opportunity for the triumphant Greeks. He even

dreams that economic prosperity will finally guarantee peaceful cohabitation between all communities: Greeks, Turks, Kurds, Jews, Arabs and Armenians.

Stavros has yet another purpose, to find a proper Anatolian girl who will give him a family. But his desire is somewhat deflected by his obsession with his former mistress ALTHEA, a blonde New York socialite who has ended their affair in order to marry PAUL, the son of Mr Fernand. A constant torment, Althea is the curse, his demon . . . and perhaps his soul mate. Stavros is convinced that Paul's fortune lured her away from him; he is equally confident that he will win her back as soon as he too becomes affluent.

During a trip to the interior of Anatolia, Stavros meets THOMNA, a spirited independent 23-year-old Greek. She has the same name as his fiancée of twenty years earlier, the girl he abandoned in Constantinople after stealing her dowry to pay for his trip to America. With Thomna he believes he can satisfy his dual longing: to establish a traditional family while remaining free to pursue Althea.

But Stavros is mistaken. Thomna is as proud and restless as he is. And she has strong emotional ties

Alexandra Stewart, Elia Kazan and Anatole Dauman

with the Turks, in particular with the nurse who
raised her after her parents' death and whose son
SALIH is now a leader of Turkish irregulars. A
childhood companion, he is in love with her. However,
Thomna dreams only of a new life in America and she
imagines that Stavros will be the one to make her
dream a reality. It is against such a backdrop of
mutual illusions that the complex relationship
between Stavros and Thomna unfolds: two rebels
discontented with their place in the world and what
seems to be their destiny.

To obtain more financing for his Anatolian
projects, Stavros joins the opportunistic Mr Fernand
in Teheran, where diplomats and adventurers are
carving up the oil market. There he is reunited with
Althea, who in his eyes personifies all that is
inaccessible and desirable about America. She
despises her husband and she has no scruples about
rekindling Stavros' passion. But she takes a
perverse pleasure in provoking and rejecting her
lover in turn. He swears that within a year he will
make a fortune and be able to offer her the luxurious
life to which she is accustomed.

In spite of his disability, Michaelis re-enlists
in the Greek army to fight the Turks, while Stavros'
obsessive desire for wealth draws him back to New
York. A year later, thanks to his intense efforts,
Mr Fernand's company controls the Oriental rug
market, with Stavros as chief executive. However,
it seems that nothing can break down Althea's
resistance.

Unaware that the Turks, under Mustapha Kemal's
leadership, have succeeded in launching a victorious
counter-offensive, Stavros goes back to Anatolia to
expand his business. The situation deteriorates
rapidly for the Greek army, Stavros is thrown in
gaol by the military for criticising the incom-
petence of the high command. He is liberated when
the Greek army flees and the countryside falls back
into Turkish hands. Concerned for his brother's
safety, Stavros begins a frantic search, running
headlong into the chaotic throngs of retreating
Greek soldiers. He stumbles into a battlefield and
there he discovers Michaelis' corpse, half devoured
by dogs.

Overwhelmed by horror and trembling with fever,
Stavros finds a refuge at Thomna's house. Attempting
to comfort the man, she lies down with him. For the
first time, they make love. Because he thinks he is

doomed to destroy all those who become attached to him, Stavros hesitates to make a commitment to Thomna. However, war forces them to flee Smyrna, for Mustapha Kemal's cavalry is already thundering down upon the city. Their only recourse is to reach the harbour in the hope of securing a boat. On the way, they encounter a group of Turkish soldiers who demand that every Greek crawl under the huge flag stretched across the street. By refusing to stoop, Thomna provokes their arrest.

Brought before the commanding officer, Stavros and Thomna discover it is Salih, Thomna's half-brother. Stavros, protected by his American citizen-ship, is released without knowing what will happen to Thomna, who remains at the mercy of Salih. While wandering about the occupied city, Stavros comes upon a Turkish mob that is lynching the Archbishop of Smyrna. When he attempts to come to his rescue, Stavros is severely beaten but manages to hide among the dock workers.

Like the Stavros of twenty years earlier on the shores of the Bosphorus, he is once again among the ranks of the 'hamals' under the rod of the stevedore. Powerless, he witnesses the torching of the city and the atrocities inflicted upon its civilians. To escape the massacre, he is forced to jump into the bay and swim toward the foreign ships which have come to evacuate their nationals. Turkish soldiers on the shore are taking potshots at the hundreds of Greeks who are trying to swim away, picking them off one by one. Stavros is rescued by American sailors as the apocalypse descends on the city.

When he finally reaches New York, Stavros dis-covers that his stock of rugs has acquired tremendous value and he resumes the life of a successful businessman. As time goes by, he marries a beautiful young American who looks like Althea. But he is still tortured by thoughts of Thomna. Is she alive? Is she a prisoner? Out of guilt, he makes it his cause to provide the Anatolian refugees in Greece with the means of resuming their traditional craft. He becomes a hero for his fellow Greeks, even though the compassion he shows his Anatolian brothers is making him richer every day . . .

Upon an invitation from the Greek government, he goes back to the islands of the Aegean Sea, to visit the refugee communities which he has provided with a livelihood. During an official ceremony on the island of Mytilini, he spots Thomna, working at a loom and rocking an infant . . .

(left to right) *Alain Robbe-Grillet, Wim Wenders, Anatole Dauman and Elia Kazan*

FILMOGRAPHY

FEATURES

Les Crimes de l'amour: Le Rideau cramoisi
France 1952. 1235m. 45 mins. b&w.
Production: Argos Films; *Director of Production*: Sacha Kamenka; *Director*: Alexandre Astruc; *Assistant Director*: Jean Leduc; *Scenario*: from the story by Barbey d'Aurevilly; *Camera*: Eugen Shuftan; *Camera Operator*: Raymond Picon-Borel; *Assistant Camera Operators*: Miklachevsky and Denis d'Ines; *Decor*: Mayo; *Production Manager*: Philippe Senne; *Costumes*: Mayo; *Dresser*: Paulette Ten-Have; *Make-up*: Jeanine Jarreau; *Editing*: Jean Mitry; *Music*: Jean-Jacques Grunenwald.
Premiere: 6 March 1953.
Prizes: Louis Delluc Prize 1952; Special Mention from the jury at Cannes 1952; Prix Fémina du cinéma; Certificate of Merit from Edinburgh 1953.
Cast: Anouk Aimée, Jean-Claude Pascal, Jim Gérald, Marguerite Garcya, Yves Furet.

Les Crimes de l'amour: Mina de Vanghel
France 1952. 1258m. 47 mins. b&w.
Production: Argos Films, Como-Films; *Production Secretary*: Yvonne Bertoni; *Director*: Maurice Clavel and Maurice Barry; *Assistant Director*: Pierre Merle; *Scenario*: Maurice Clavel, Georges Rouquier and Maurice Barry, from Stendhal; *Dialogues and text*: Maurice Clavel; *Commentary* spoken by Michel Bouquet; *Camera*: Eugen Shuftan; *Camera Operator*: Picon-Borel; *Assistant Camera Operators*: Mick and Denis d'Ines; *Sound*: René Lécuyer; *Sound Assistant*: M. Chantreuil; *Decor*: Mayo; *Decorator*: Alexis de Giers; *Assistant Decorator*: J.J. Gambut; *Script girl*: Colette Thiriet; *Costumes*: Mayo; *Editing*: Madeleine Bagiau and Yannick Bellon; *Assistant Editor*: J. Hubert; *Music*: Jean-Jacques Grunenwald.
Premiere: 6 March 1953.
Cast: Odile Versois, Marie Sabouret, Alain Cuny, Jean Servais, Yvonne Yma.

Lettre de Sibérie (Impressions de voyage)
France 1958. 1826m. 67 mins. colour.
Production: Argos Films, Procinex; *Executive Producer*: Anatole Dauman; *Director*: Chris Marker; *Documentation*: Armand Gatti; *Camera*: Sacha Vierny; *Recitation*: Georges Rouquier; *Editing*: Chris Marker; *Assistant Editor*: Anne Sarraute; *Music*:

Pierre Barbaud; *Music Director*: Georges Delerue.
Premiere: 1 November 1958.
Prize: Lumière Prize 1958.

Hiroshima mon amour
France 1959. 2489m. 91 mins. b&w.
Production: Argos Films, Como-Films, DAIEI Motion Picture Co. Ltd, Pathé
Overseas Productions; *Production Directors*: Sacha Kamenka, Shirakawa Takeo;
Director: Alain Resnais; *Assistant Directors*: Tanneguy Andréfouet, Jean-Pierre
Léon, René Guyonnet, I. Shirai, Itoi, Hara; *Scenario and dialogues*: Marguerite
Duras; *Camera*: Sacha Vierny and Takahashi Mishio; *Assistant Camera Operators*:
Pierre Goupil, Watanabe, Ioda; *Sound*: Pierre Calvet, Yamamoto, René Renault;
Decors: Esaka, Mayo, Petri; *Script girl*: Sylvette Baudrot; *Production Managers*:
R. Knabe, I. Obashi; *Costumes*: Gérard Collery; *Editing*: Henri Colpi, Jasmine
Chasney, Anne Sarraute; *Music*: Giovanni Fusco, Georges Delerue.
Cast: Emmanuèle Riva, Eiji Okada, Bernard Fresson, Stella Dassas, Pierre
Barbaud.
Premiere: 10 June 1959.
Prizes: FIPRESCI Prize; Prize of The Society of Film and Television Writers at
Cannes 1959; New York Critics' Prize 1960; New York Distributors' Prize 1960.
Literary Consultant: Gérard Jarlot.

Chronique d'un été
France 1960. 2441m. 90 mins. b&w.
Production: Argos Films; *Executive Producer*: Anatole Dauman; *Production Direc-
tor*: André Heinrich; *Directors*: Jean Rouch and Edgar Morin; *Assistant Directors*:
Claude Beausoleil and Louis Boucher; *Camera*: Roger Morillère, Raoul Coutard,
Jean-Jacques Tarbes; Michel Brault; *Sound*: Guy Rophé, Michel Fano, Edmond
Barthélémy; *Editing*: Jean Ravel, Nena Baratier, Françoise Colin.
Premiere: 20 October 1961.
Prizes: International Critics' Prize at Cannes 1961; Pasinetti Prize; Ciné Forum
Prize at Venice; First Prize at Mannheim 1961; Quality Prize at the Festival dei
popoli in Florence.
Cast: Marceline, Mary-Lou, Angelo, Jean-Pierre; workers: Jacques, Jean; stu-
dents: Régis, Céline, Jean-Marc, Nadine, Landry, Raymond; employees: Jacques,
Simone; artists: Henri, Madi, Catherine; cover girl: Sophie, and unknown people
encountered in Paris.

L'Année dernière à Marienbad (*Last Year at Marienbad*)
France/Italy 1961. 2544m. 93 mins. b&w. Dyaliscope.
Production: Terra Films, Argos Films, Films Tamara, Cinetel, Silver Films
(France), Cineriz (Rome), Como-Films, Cormoran, Précitel; *Executive Produ-
cers*: Pierre Coureau and Pierre Froment; *Production Director*: Léon Sanz;
Director: Alain Resnais; *Assistant Directors*: Jean Léon, Volker Schlöndorff,
Florence Malraux; *Original scenario and dialogues*: Alain Robbe-Grillet; *Camera*:

Sacha Vierny; *Framing*: Philippe Brun; *Sound*: Guy Villette, Jean-Claude Marchetti, René Renault, Jean Neny, Robert Cambourakis; *Decors*: Jacques Saulnier; *Script girl*: Sylvette Baudrot; *Production Manager*: Michel Choquet; *Costumes*: Delphine Seyrig's dresses by Chanel; *Make-up*: Alexandre and Éliane Marcus; *Editing*: Henri Colpi and Jasmine Chasney; *Music*: Francis Seyrig (organ player: Marie-Louise Girod).
Premiere: 27 September 1961.
Prizes: Golden Lion at Venice 1961; Méliès Prize.
Cast: Delphine Seyrig, Giorgio Albertazzi, Sacha Pitoëff, Françoise Bertin, Luce Garcia-Ville, Héléna Kornel, Françoise Spira, Karin Toeche Mittler, Jean Lanier, Pierre Barbaud, Wilhelm von Deek, Gérard Lorin, David Montemury, Gilles Quéant, Gabriel Werner.

Le Rendez-vous de minuit
France 1961. 2723m. 100 mins. b&w.
Production: Argos Films, les Films du Compas, Les Éditions cinématographiques, Films Roger Leenhardt; *Production Director*: Philippe Dussart; *Executive Producer*: Jean Thuillier; *Production Assistant*: Olga Waren; *Director*: Roger Leenhardt; *Assistant Director*: Didier Goulard; *Scenario*: Roger Leenhardt in collaboration with Jean-Pierre Vivet; *Camera*: Jean Badal; *Camera Operator*: Jean Charvein; *Assistant Operator*: Étienne Szabo; *Sound*: André Hervée; *Decors*: Bernard Evein; *Assistant Decorator*: Marc Frederix; *Editing*: Henri Lanoë; *Assistant Editor*: Jacqueline Meppiel; *Music*: Georges Auric; *Make-up*: Jackie Reynal; *Hairdresser*: Simone Knapp.
Premiere: 30 May 1962.
Cast: Lilli Palmer; Michel Auclair, France Anglade, Lucienne Lemarchand, Robert Lombard, Michel de Ré, Michèle Meritz, Olga Wassily, Bruno Balp, Marcel Charvey, Daniel Emilfork, Jean Galland, Alvaro Gheri, José Luis de Villalonga, with the participation of Maurice Ronet.

Muriel or *Le Temps d'un retour*
France/Italy 1962. 2700m. 99 mins. Eastmancolor.
Production: Argos Films, Dear Films (Rome), Alpha Productions; *Executive Producer*: Anatole Dauman; *Production Director*: Philippe Dussart; *Director*: Alain Resnais; *Assistant Directors*: Jean Léon, Pierre Grünstein; *Trainee*: Florence Malraux; *Scenario and dialogues*: Jean Cayrol; *Camera*: Sacha Vierny; *Framing*: Philippe Brun; *Sound*: Antoine Bonfanti; *Sound Assistants*: Jean Philippe, Jean Gaudelet; *Mixing*: Jean Neny; *Decors*: Jacques Saulnier, Charles Merangel; *Script girl*: Sylvette Baudrot; *Production Manager*: Michel Choquet; *Make-up*: Alex and Éliane Marcus; *Editing*: Kenout Peltier and Éric Pluet; *Assistant Editors*: Claudine Merlin, Svelta Fingova; *Music*: Hans Werner Henze; *Conductor*: Georges Delerue.
Premiere: 2 October 1963.
Prizes: Volpi Cup for Best Actress, International Critics' Prize and Unicrit Prize at Venice 1963; Sutherland Trophy in London 1963.

Cast: Delphine Seyrig, Jean-Pierre Kerien, Nita Klein, Jean-Baptiste Thierrée, Claude Sainval, Jean Champion, Laurence Badie, Martine Vatel, Philippe Laudenbach, Jean Dasté, Robert Bordenave, Gaston Joly, Nelly Borgeaud, Julien Verdier, Catherine de Seynes, Gérard Lorin, Françoise Bertin, Wanda Kerien, Jean-Jacques Lagarde, Paul Chevallier, Laure Paillette, Éliane Chevet, Yves Vincent.

Demain la Chine
(consisting of: *Le Mystère Mao, Un immense visage, 700 millions*)
France 1965. 2197m. 80 mins. b&w and colour.
Production: Argos Films; *Director*: Claude Otzenberger; *Commentary*: Christophe Berger (Chris Marker ?); *Camera*: Michel Parbot; *Sound*: Harold Maury; *Editing*: Ragnar.
Premiere: 14 September 1966.
Prize: Golden Ducat at Mannheim 1966.

Au hasard Balthazar
France/Sweden 1966. 2611m. 96 mins. b&w.
Production: Argos Films, Parc Film, Athos Films, Swedish Film Institute, Svensk Filmindustri (Stockholm); *Production Director*: Philippe Dussart; *Director*: Robert Bresson; *Assistant Directors*: Jacques Kebadian, Sven Frostenson, Claude Miller; *Scenario and adaptation*: Robert Bresson; *Camera*: Ghislain Cloquet; *Camera Operator*: Jean Chiabaut; *Sound*: Antoine Archimbaud, Jacques Carrère; *Decors*: Pierre Charbonnier; *Script girl*: Geneviève Cortier; *Production Manager*: Michel Choquet; *Editing*: Raymond Lamy and Geneviève Billo; *Music*: Schubert's Sonata no. 20 played by Jean-Noël Barbier), Jean Wiener (jazz).
Premiere: 10 May 1966.
Prizes: Georges Méliès Prize; OCIC First Prize together with a Unanimous Tribute by the Jury, the San Giorgio Prize, the Pasinetti Prize, the Cineforum Prize and the Cinema nuovo Prize, all at Venice 1966; First Prize at the Journées du Capitole in Rome; Special Jury Prize at the 4th International Festival of Panama.
Cast: Anne Wiazemski, François Lafarge, Philippe Asselin, Nathalie Joyaut, Walter Green, J.C. Guilbert, Pierre Klossowski, François Sullerot, M.C. Frémont, Jean Rémignard, Jacques Sorbets, Tord Paag, Sven Frostenson, Roger Fjellstrom, Jean-Noël Barbier, Remy Brozeck, Mylène Weyergans, Guy Brejac.

Le désordre a vingt ans
(consisting of: *Désordre* and *Voilà l'ordre*)
France 1966. 1930m. 70 mins. b&w.
Production: Argos Films, S.N. Pathé Cinéma; *Director*: Jacques Baratier; *Assistant Directors*: Marie Caban and Bernard Maréchal; *Camera*: Étienne Becker; *Sound*: Jean-Claude Loreux; *Editing*: Marie-Françoise Thomas.
Premiere: 19 September 1967.
Cast: Antonin Artaud, Jacques Audiberti, Arthur Adamov, Simone de Beauvoir,

Roger Blin, Albert Camus, César, François Dufrêne, Danièle Delorme, Marcel Duhamel, Duke Ellington, Juliette Gréco, Daniel Gélin, Guillaume Hanoteau, Isidore Isou, Robert Kanters, Claude Luter, Claude Nougaro, Marcello Pagliero, Jacques Prévert, Pierre Prévert, Raymond Queneau, Michel de Ré, Jean-Paul Sartre, Roger Vadim, Boris Vian . . .

Deux ou trois choses que je sais d'elle (*Two or Three Things I Know About Her*)
France 1966. 2380m. 87 mins. Scope; Eastmancolor.
Production: Argos Films, Parc Film, les Films du Carrosse, Anouchka Films; *Executive Producer*: Philippe Dussart; *Production Director*: Philippe Senne; *Director*: Jean-Luc Godard; *Assistant Directors*: Charles Bitsch (1st), Isabelle Pons (2nd); *Trainee Director*: Robert Chevassu; *Scenario*: Jean-Luc Godard from an investigation published by *Le Nouvel Observateur*; *Documentation*: Catherine Vimenet; *Camera*: Raoul Coutard; *Camera Operator*: Georges Liron; *Assistant Camera Operator*: Jean Garcenot; *Sound*: René Levert; *Boom*: Robert Cambourakis; *Script girl*: Suzanne Schiffman; *Production Manager*: Claude Miller; *Costumes*: Gitt Magrini; *Dresser*: Dora Balabanow; *Make-up*: Jackie Reynal; *Hairdressing*: Renée Guidet; *Editing*: Françoise Collin; *Music*: Beethoven Quartet.
Premiere: 18 March 1967 (over 18 only).
Prizes: Fémina Prize 1967; Marilyn Monroe Prize 1967.
Cast: Marina Vlady, Anny Duperey, Roger Montsoret, Jean Narboni, Christophe and Marie Bourseiller, Joseph Gehrard, Raoul Lévy, Helena Bielicic, Robert Chevassu, Yves Beneyton, Jean-Pierre Laverne, Blandine Jeanson, Claude Miller, Jean-Patrick Lebel, Juliet Berto, Anna Manga, Benjamin Rosette, Helen Scott.

Masculin-féminin
France/Sweden 1966. 2901m. 106 mins. b&w.
Production: Argos Films, Anouchka Films, Svensk Filmindustri, Sandrews (Stockholm); *Executive Producer*: Philippe Dussart; *Production Director*: Philippe Dussart; *Director*: Jean-Luc Godard; *Assistant Directors*: Bernard Toublanc-Michel and Jacques-Henri Barratier; *Scenario*: Jean-Luc Godard, freely adapted from two stories by Maupassant (*La Femme de Paul* and *Le Signe*); *Camera*: Willy Kurant; *Assistant Camera Operator*: William Lubtchansky; *Sound*: René Levert; *Script girl*: Élisabeth Rappeneau; *Editing*: Agnès Guillemot; *Music*: Mozart, Francis Lai.
Premiere: 18 April 1966.
Prizes: Silver Bear at Berlin 1966; Prize for the Youth Film by the Senate of Berlin; Interfilm Jury Special Mention.
Cast: Marlène Jobert, Jean-Pierre Léaud, Chantal Goya, Michel Debord, Catherine-Isabelle Duport, Eva Britt Strandberg, Birger Malmsten, Elsa Leroy, Françoise Hardy, Brigitte Bardot, Antoine Bourseiller, Chantal Darget.

Mona l'étoile sans nom
France/Romania 1966. 2425m. 89 mins. b&w.
Production: Argos Films, Films Luciana, Cocinor, Films Marceau, Centrul de

Producti Cinematografica (Bucharest); *Executive Producer*: Anatole Dauman; *Director*: Henri Colpi; *Scenario*: Henri Colpi from the play by Mikhaïl Sebastian; *Camera*: Aurel Samson; *Music*: Georges Delerue.
Premiere: 18 October 1966.
Cast: Marina Vlady, Claude Rich, Christ Avram, Héléna Popivici, Birlic.

17e parallèle
(consisting of: *La Guerre du peuple, Agrippés à la terre, Déterminés à vaincre*)
France/Vietnam 1967. 3246m. 119 mins. b&w.
Production: Argos Films, Capi Film, Hanoi Documentary Studios; *Director*: Joris Ivens in collaboration with Marceline Loridan.
Premiere: 6 March 1968.
With the collaboration of Bui Dinh Hac, Nguyen Thi, Huan Phuong, Nguyen Quang Tuan, Dao Le Binh, Pham Chon, Liliane Korb, Maguy Alziari, Phuong Batho, Jean-Pierre Sergent, Dang Vu Bich Lien, Jean Neny, Antoine Bonfanti, Pierre Angles, Michel Fano, Harald Maury, Donald Sturbelle, André Van der Beken, Bernard Ortion, Georges Loiseau.

Mouchette
France 1967. 2207m. 81 mins. b&w.
Production: Argos Films, Parc Film; *Executive Producer*: Anatole Dauman; *Production Directors*: Philippe Dussart and Michel Choquet; *Director*: Robert Bresson; *Assistant Directors*: Jacques Kebadian and Mylène Van der Mersch; *Scenario*: Robert Bresson from *Nouvelle histoire de Mouchette* by Georges Bernanos; *Camera*: Ghislain Cloquet; *Camera Operator*: Jean Chiabaut; *Assistant Camera Operators*: Emmanuel Machuel, Paul Bonis; *Sound*: Séverin Frankiel and Jacques Carrère; *Sound Effects*: Daniel Couteau; *Decors*: Pierre Guffroy; *Script girl*: Françoise Renberg; *Production Manager*: René Pascal; *Dresser*: Odette Le Barbenchon; *Editing*: Raymond Lamy; *Assistant Editor*: Arlette Lalande; *Music*: Monteverdi's 'Magnificat', Jean Wiener (song and fair music).
Premiere: 15 March 1967.
Prizes: Unanimous Tribute from the Jury and the OCIC Prize at Cannes 1967; Inter-Club du cinéma Prize 1967; First Prize at Panama Festival, 1966; Best Actress Prize at Panama 1966 to Nadine Nortier.
Cast: Nadine Nortier, Jean-Claude Guilbert, Marie Cardinal, Paul Hébert, Jean Vimenet, Marie Susini, Liliane Princet, Raymonde Chabrun, Martine Trichet, Suzanne Huguenin.

Tu imagines Robinson (Oniros)
France 1967. 2450m. 90 mins. Eastmancolor.
Production: Les Films du Losange, Argos Films; *Director*: Jean-Daniel Pollet; *Monologue*: Remo Forlani; *Narrative Text*: Jean Thibaudeau; *Camera*: Yan Lemasson; *Editing*: Françoise Geissler.
Premiere: 12 December 1968.
Prize: Best Actor at Trieste 1969.
Cast: Tobias Engels, Maria Limaria.

L'amour c'est gai, l'amour c'est triste
France 1968. 2465m. 90 mins. Eastmancolor.
Production: Argos Films, Galba Film; *Executive Producer*: Anatole Dauman; *Production Director*: Anatole Dauman; *Director*: Jean-Daniel Pollet; *Assistant Director*: Pierre Beuchot; *Scenario*: Jean-Daniel Pollet and Remo Forlani; *Dialogues*: Remo Forlani; *Camera*: Jean-Jacques Rochut; *Sound*: René Levert; *Mixing*: Antoine Bonfanti; *Costumes*: Jenny Pollet; *Editing*: Nena Baratier; *Music*: Jean-Jacques Debout.
Premiere: 26 March 1971.
Cast: Claude Melki, Bernadette Lafont, Jean-Pierre Marielle, Dalio, Chantal Goya, Christian de Tillières, Jacques Doniol-Valcroze, Remo Forlani.

Les Deux Marseillaises
(consisting of: *Marseillaise I, Marseillaise II* (*Urbanité 68*))
France 1968. 2982m. 109 mins. b&w.
Production: Argos Films; *Directors*: André S. Labarthe and Jean-Louis Comolli; *Assistant Directors*: Luc Béraud, Claude Massot and Robert Amar; *Camera*: Philippe Théaudière, Jean-Yves Coïc, Daniel Cardot; *Sound*: Students from the IDHEC; *Editing*: Cécile Decugis; Lise Beaulieu and Dominique Villain.
Premiere: 28 November 1968.

Contes immoraux (*Immoral Tales*)
(consisting of: *La Marée* from a story by André Pieyre de Mandiargues, *Thérèse philosophe, Erszebet Báthory, Lucrezia Borgia*)
France 1974. 2847m. 104 mins. Eastmancolor.
Production: Argos Films; *Director*: Walerian Borowczyk; *Assistant Director*: Dominique Duvergé; *Scenario*: Walerian Borowczyk; *Camera*: Bernard Daillencourt, Guy Durban, Michel Zolat, Noël Véry; *Sound*: Pierre Delagarde; *Decors*: W. Borowczyk; *Costumes*: Piet Bolscher; *Editing*: Anne-Marie Sachs; *Music*: Maurice Le Roux.
Premiere: 28 August 1974 (over 18 only).
Prize: L'Age d'Or Prize in Brussels 1974.
Cast: Paloma Picasso, Pascale Christophe, Charlotte Alexandra, Lise Danvers, Fabrice Luchini, Florence Bellamy, Jacopo Berinizi, Lorenzo Berinizi.

La Bête
France 1975. 2837m. 104 mins. Eastmancolor.
Production: Argos Films; *Production Director*: Dominique Duvergé; *Director*: Walerian Borowczyk; *Assistant Director*: Christiane Regnault; *Scenario*: Walerian Borowczyk; *Camera*: Bernard Daillencourt and Marcel Grignon; *Sound*: Jean-Pierre Ruh; *Decors*: Jacques d'Ovidio and Alain Guillé; *Costumes*: Piet Bolscher; *Editing*: Henri Colpi.
Premiere: 20 August 1975 (over 18 only).
Cast: Sirpa Lane, Lisbeth Hummel, Pierre Benedetti, Dalio, Guy Tréjean, Roland Armontel, Pascale Rivault, Jean Martinelli, Robert Capia.

Chantons sous l'Occupation
France 1976. 2380m. 87 mins. b&w and colour.
Production: Argos Films, Les Films Armorial, Institute national de l'audiovisuel; *Executive Producers*: Simon Damiani, André Valio-Caraglione; *Director*: André Halimi; *Camera* (contemporary images): Jean Rouch; *Sound*: Vincent Blanchet; *Editing*: Henri Colpi.
Premiere: 27 April 1976.
With: Jean-Louis Barrault, Marie Bell, Pierre Blanchar, Danielle Darrieux, Suzy Delair, Maurice Chevalier, Mistinguett, Charles Trenet, Marcel Cerdan, Sacha Guitry, Jean-Louis Bory, Édith Piaf, Jules Berry, Tino Rossi . . .

Le Coup de grâce (Der Fangschuss)
France/Germany 1976. 2639m. 97 mins. b&w.
Production: Argos Films, Bioskop Film (Munich); *Executive Producer*: Eberhard Junkersdorf; *Director*: Volker Schlöndorff; *Scenario and dialogues*: Geneviève Dormann, Margarethe von Trotta and Jutta Bruckner from the novel by Marguerite Yourcenar; *Camera*: Igor Luther; *Sound*: Gerhard Birkholz and Willi Schwadorf; *Decor*: Hans-Jürgen Kiebach; *Editing*: Jane Sperr and Annette Dom with the collaboration of Henri Colpi; *Music*: Stanley Myers.
Premiere: 17 November 1976.
Prize: First Prize at Naples Festival.
Cast: Matthias Habich, Margarethe von Trotta, Mathieu Carrière, Valeska Gert, Rüdiger Kirchstein, Marc Eyraud, Frederik Zichy, Bruno Thost, Henry Van Lyck.

L'Empire des sens (Ai no corrida/Empire of the Senses)
France/Japan 1976. 3023m. 102 mins. Eastmancolor.
Production: Argos Films, Oshima Productions Tokyo; *Executive Producer*: Anatole Dauman; *Production Director*: Koji Wakamatsu; *Director*: Nagisa Oshima; *Scenario*: Nagisa Oshima; *Camera*: Hideo Ito; *Sound*: Tetsuo Yasuda; *Lighting*: Kenichi Okamoto; *Decor and Costumes*: Jusho Toda; *Editing*: Keiichi Uraoka; *Music*: Minoru Miki.
Premiere: 15 September 1976 (over 18 only).
Prize: First Prize at Chicago International Festival, 1976; Best Film of the Year in London 1976.
Cast: Eiko Matsuda and Tatsuya Fuji.

L'Empire de la passion (Ai no borei/Empire of Passion)
France/Japan 1978. 2912m. 108 mins. Eastmancolor.
Production: Argos Films, Oshima Productions Tokyo; *Production Director*: Shigeru Wakatsuki; *Director*: Nagisa Oshima; *Scenario*: Nagisa Oshima from a story by Mme Itoko Nakamura; *Camera*: Yoshio Miyajima; *Sound*: Tetsuo Yasuda and Alex Pront; *Lighting*: Kenichi Okamoto; *Decor*: Jusho Toda; *Editing*: Keiichi Uraoka; *Music*: Toru Takemitsu.
Premiere: 6 September 1978 (over 18 only).

Prize: Best Direction Prize at Cannes 1978.
Cast: Kazuko Yoshiyuki, Tatsuya Fuji, Akiko Koyama, Taiji Tonoyama, Taka-
hiro Tamura, Takuzo Kawatani, Sumie Sasaki, Eizo Kitamura, Masami Hase-
gawa, Kenzo Kawarazaki, Takaki Sugiura.

Le Tambour (Die Blechtrommel/The Tin Drum)
France/Germany 1979. 3883m. 142 mins. Eastmancolor.
Production: Argos Films, Franz Seitz Film (Munich), Bioskop Film, Artemis
Film; *Executive Producers*: Franz Seitz and Anatole Dauman; *Production Director*:
Eberhard Junkersdorf; *Director*: Volker Schlöndorff; *Scenario*: Jean-Claude Car-
rière, Volker Schlöndorff, Franz Seitz from the novel by Günter Grass; *Art
Director*: Nicos Perakis; *Camera*: Igor Luther; *Special Effects*: Georges Iaconelli;
Decor: Bernard Lepel; *Editing*: Suzanne Baron; *Music*: Maurice Jarre.
Premiere: 19 September 1979.
Prizes: Golden Palm at Cannes 1979; Oscar for the Best Foreign Film in 1980.
Cast: David Bennent, Mario Adorf, Angela Winkler, Daniel Olbrychski, Andrea
Ferreol, Charles Aznavour, Katharina Tahlbach, Heinz Bennent, Fritz Hakl,
Mariella Oliveri, Tina Engel, Berta Drews, Roland Teubner, Ernst Jacobi,
Wigand Witting, Marek Walczewski, Wojcech Pszoniak, Otto Sander, Karl-
Heinz Tittelbach, Emil F. Feist, Herbert Behrent, Bruno Thost, Gerda Blisse,
Joachim Hackethal, Zygmunt Huebner, Mieczyslaw Czechowicz.

Elia Kazan outsider
France 1981. 615m. in 16mm. 56 mins. colour.
Production: Argos Films; *Director*: Annie Tresgot; *Interviewer*: Michel Ciment;
Camera: Michel Brault; *Sound*: Dominique Chartrand; *Editing*: François Ceppi.
Premiere: 15 September 1982.
With: Elia Kazan, Robert De Niro, Tommy Bull, Eileen Shanahan, Mike Kazan.

Le Faussaire (Die Fälschung/Circle of Deceit)
France/Germany 1981. 2985m. 110 mins. colour.
Production: Argos Films, Bioskop Film (Munich), Artemis Film; *Executive
Producer*: Eberhard Junkersdorf; *Production Director*: Herbert Kerz; *Director*:
Volker Schlöndorff; *Assistant Director*: Régis Wargnier; *Scenario*: Volker Schlön-
dorff, Jean-Claude Carrière, Margarethe von Trotta, Kai Hermann from the
novel by Nicolas Born; *Camera*: Igor Luther; *Special Effects*: Paul and André
Trielli; *Sound*: Christian Moldt, Helmut Rottgen, Christian Schubert; *Decor*:
Bernd Lepel, Jacques Bufnoir; *Costumes*: Dagmar Niefind; *Editing*: Suzanne
Baron; *Music*: Maurice Jarre.
Premiere: 28 October 1981.
Cast: Bruno Ganz, Hanna Schygulla, Jean Carmet, Jerzy Skolimowski, Gila von
Weitershausen, Peter Martin Urtcl, John Munro, Fouad Naïm, Josette Khalil,
Khaled El Saeid, Ghassan Mattar, Sarah Salem, Tafic Najem, Magnia Fakhoury,
Jack Diagilaitas.

Les Fruits de la passion (*Shanghai ijin shokan*/*The Fruits of Passion*)
France/Japan 1981. 2254m. 82 mins. colour.
Production: Argos Films, Terayama Productions, Launoy Films; *Production Director*: Kiyoshi Nishiura; *Associate Producers*: Jacques-Henri Barratier, Philippe d'Argilat; *Director*: Shuji Terayama; *Scenario*: Shuji Terayama from Pauline Réage's *Retour à Roissy*; *Voice-off Narration*: Pauline Réage; *Camera*: Tatsuo Suzuki; *Sound*: Yukio Kubota; *Decor*: Hiroshi Yamashita; *Costumes*: Kaisik Wong; *Make-up and Hairdressing*: Sachiko Kawabe; *Editing*: Henri Colpi; *Music*: J.A. Seazer.
Premiere: 2 June 1981 (over 18 only).
Cast: Klaus Kinski, Isabelle Illiers, Arielle Dombasle, Keiko Niitaka, Sayoko Yamaguchi.

La Belle Captive
France 1982. 2417m. 90 mins. colour.
Production: Argos Films; *Production Director*: Bernard Bouix; *Director*: Alain Robbe-Grillet; *Assistant Director*: Richard Malbequi; *Scenario*: Alain Robbe-Grillet; *Camera*: Henri Alekan; *Framing*: Noël Very; *Decors*: Aimé Deude; *Assistant Decorator*: Gilles Roland-Guerber; *Costumes*: Piet Bolscher; *Sound Effects*: Jacques Tassel; *Mixing*: Jack Jullian; *Editing*: Bob Wade; *Sound Engineer*: Gérard Barra; *Music*: 15th Schubert Quartet and 'The Mooch' by Duke Ellington.
Premiere: 16 February 1983.
Cast: Daniel Mesguich, Cyrielle Claire, Daniel Emilfork, François Chaumette, Gabrielle Lazure.

Sans soleil (*Sunless*)
France 1982. 2736m. 100 mins. colour.
Production: Argos Films; *Director*: Chris Marker; *Assistant Director*: Pierre Camus; *Scenario and texts*: Chris Marker; *Voices*: Alexandra Stewart (English version), Florence Delay (French version); *Camera*: Chris Marker; *Editing*: Chris Marker; *Assistant Editors*: Anne-Marie L'Hote, Catherine Adda; *Music*: Michel Krasna; *Song*: Arielle Dombasle; *Mixing*: Antoine Bonfanti, Paul Bertault.
Premiere: 2 March 1983.
Prizes: International Critics Prize at the London Film Festival of 1983; First Prize at the Festival dei popoli in Florence 1983; British Film Institute Award in London 1983.

Paris, Texas
France/Germany 1984. 3970m. 145 mins. colour.
Production: Argos Films, Road Movies (Berlin); *Producer*: Chris Sievernich; *Executive Producer*: Anatole Dauman; *Associate Producer*: Pascale Dauman; *Director*: Wim Wenders; *Assistant Director*: Claire Denis; *Scenario*: Sam Shepard; *Adaptation*: L.M. Kit Carson, Bernard Eisenschitz; *Camera*: Robby Müller; *Camera Assistants*: Agnès Godard, Pim Tjuerman; *Sound*: Jean-Paul Mugel; *Boom*: Douglas Axtell; *Mixing*: Hartmut Eichgrün; *Art Direction*: Kate Altman;

Assistant Art Direction: Lorrie Brown; *Costumes*: Brigitta Byerke; *Script girl*: Helen Caldwell; *Production Manager*: Karen Koch; *Editing*: Peter Przygodda; *Music*: Ry Cooder.
Premiere: 19 September 1984.
Prizes: Golden Palm, International Critics Prize, French Critics Association Prize and the Ecumenical Jury Prize at Cannes 1984.
Cast: Harry Dean Stanton, Dean Stockwell, Aurore Clément, Nastassja Kinski, Hunter Carson, Sam Berry, Bernhard Wicki, Claresie Mobley, Viva Auder, Socorro Valdez, Justin Hogg, Edward Fayton, Tom Farrell, John Lurie, Jeni Vici, Sally Norvell, Sharon Menzel, The Mydolls.

Le Sacrifice (*Offret/ The Sacrifice*)
France/Sweden 1986. 3987m. 155 mins. colour.
Production: Swedish Film Institute (Stockholm), Argos Films; *Production Director*: Katinka Faragò; *Executive Producer*: Anna-Lena Wibom; *Director*: Andrei Tarkovsky; *Assistant Director*: Kerstin Eriksdotter; *Scenario*: Andrei Tarkovsky; *Camera*: Sven Nykvist; *Camera Operators*: Lars Karlsson, Dan Myhrman; *Decor*: Anna Asp; *Editing*: Andrei Tarkovsky, Michal Leszczylowski; *Technical Adviser to the editors*: Henri Colpi; *Music*: J. S. Bach; *Script girl*: Anne von Sydow; *Costumes*: Inger Pehrson; *Make-up and hairdressing*: Kjell Gustavsson, Florence Fouquier; *Sound and Mixing*: Owe Swenson, Bo Persson, Lars Ulander, Christin Loman, Wille Peterson Berger; *Production Manager*: Göran Lindberg, Agneta Jansson.
Premiere: 14 May 1986.
Prizes: Special Jury Prize, Prize for Artistic Achievement, International Critics Prize and the Ecumenical Jury Prize at Cannes 1986; Orson Welles Prize 1987.
Cast: Erland Josephson, Susan Fleetwood, Valérie Mairesse, Allan Edwall, Gudrun S. Gisladottir, Sven Wollter, Filippa Franzén, Tommy Kjellqvist, Per Källman, Tommy Nordahl.

Les Ailes du désir (*Der Himmel über Berlin/ Wings of Desire*)
France/Germany 1987. 3502m. 126 mins. b&w and colour.
Production: Argos Films, Road Movies; *Producers*: Wim Wenders, Anatole Dauman; *Production Director*: Ingrid Windisch; *Associate Producers*: Joachim von Mengershausen, Pascale Dauman; *Director*: Wim Wenders; *Assistant Directors*: Claire Denis, Knut Winckler; *Scenario*: Wim Wenders in collaboration with Peter Handke; *Camera*: Henri Alekan; *Camera Operator*: Agnès Godard; *Assistant Camera Operator*: Louis Cochet; *Sound*: Jean-Paul Mugel and Axel Arft; *Sound Transfer*: Lothar Mankewitz; *Mixing*: Hartmut Eichgrun; *Sculptor*: Claude Lalanne; *Script girl*: Gabi Mattner; *Wim Wenders' Personal Assistant*: Ulla Zwicker; *Costumes*: Monika Jacobs; *Art Direction*: Heidi Ludi; *Assistant Art Direction*: Werner Mooser; *Editing*: Peter Przygodda; *Assistant Editors*: Anne Schnee, Leni Savietto-Putz; *Music*: Jürgen Knieper.
Premiere: 16 September 1987.
Prize: Best Direction Prize at Cannes 1987.
Cast: Bruno Ganz, Solveig Dommartin, Otto Sander, Curt Bois, Peter Falk.

SHORT FILMS

1950: *Fêtes galantes* by Jean Aurel, 16 mins.
1951: *L'Affaire Manet* by Jean Aurel, 21 mins.
1952: *Les Désastres de la guerre* (*Goya*) by Pierre Kast (and J. Grémillon), 20 mins.
 Images pour Debussy (*Reflets dans l'eau* and *1re arabesque*) by Jean Mitry, 13 mins.
 Le Cœur d'amour épris du roi René by Jean Aurel, 17 mins.
 En bateau by Jean Mitry, 13 mins.
 Rêverie de Claude Debussy by Jean Mitry, 13 mins.
 Le Rideau cramoisi by Alexandre Astruc, 50 mins.
1953: *Bruegel l'ancien* by Arcady, Edmond Lévy and Gérard Pignol, 21 mins.
 Mina de Vanghel by Maurice Clavel and Maurice Barry, 45 mins.
1954: *Martin et Gaston* by Henri Gruel, 12 mins. (co-prod. Films de la Rose Rouge).
 Le Mystère de la Licorne by Jean-Claude See and Arcady, 13 mins.
1955: *Les Essais* by Jean-Gabriel Albicocco, 13 mins (co-prod. Cannes Films Prod.).
 Nuit et brouillard by Alain Resnais, 31 mins.
 Paris la nuit by Jacques Baratier and Jean Valère, 23 mins.
 Regina Caeli by Paul Haesaert and Arcady, 13 mins (co-prod. Films P.H. [Brussels]).
 La Rose et le radis by Henri Gruel, 10 mins.
 Symphonie mécanique by Jean Mitry, 13 mins.
 Une ville qu'on appelle Paris by Jean Prat, 13 mins (co-prod. ORTF).
 Le Voyage de Badabou by Henri Gruel, 10 mins.
1956: *Dimanche à Pékin* by Chris Marker, 10 mins (co-prod. Pavox Film).
 Le Voyageur by Henri Gruel, 9 mins.
1957: *Barna Senese* by Jacques Laval, 14 mins.
 Broadway by Light (*Les Lumières de Broadway*) by William Klein, 10 mins.
 La Déroute by Ado Kyrou (and Georges Franju), 14 mins.
 La Joconde by Henri Gruel, 14 mins.
 Le Jugement dernier (de Michel-Ange) by Jacques Laval, 10 mins.
 Notre-Dame, cathédrale de Paris by Georges Franju, 15 mins.
 La première nuit by Georges Franju, 20 mins.
1958: *La Cocotte d'Azur* by Agnès Varda, 10 mins.
 Les Hommes de la baleine by Mario Ruspoli, 24 mins (co-prod. Armorial).
 Images des mondes perdus by Philippe Lifchitz, 14 mins.
1959: *Les Astronautes* by Walerian Borowczyk and Chris Marker, 14 mins (co-prod. Armorial).
 Du côté de la Côte by Agnès Varda, 26 mins.
 L'Horrible, bizarre et incroyable histoire de M. Tête by Jan Lenica and Henri Gruel, 13 mins.

1960: *On vous parle* by Jean Cayrol and Claude Durand, 16 mins.
  Paris la belle by Pierre and Jacques Prévert and Marcel Duhamel, 24 mins.
  X.Y.Z. by Philippe Lifchitz, 11 mins.
1961: *Les Inconnus de la terre* (Ex: *Toi, l'Auvergnat*) by Mario Ruspoli, 40 mins.
  Madame se meurt by Jean Cayrol and Claude Durand, 17 mins.
  Regard sur la folie by Mario Ruspoli, 35 mins.
1962: *De tout pour faire un monde* by Jean Cayrol and Claude Durand, 15 mins (co-prod. Service Recherches ORTF).
  La Fête prisonnière (Ex: *Les Portes de la raison*) by Mario Ruspoli, 18 mins.
  La Jetée by Chris Marker, 26 mins.
  M. Albert prophète by Jean Rouch, 22 mins.
1963: *A Valparaiso* by Joris Ivens, 33 mins.
  Le Petit Chapiteau by Joris Ivens, 7 mins.
1964: *A* by Jan Lenica, 9 mins.
  Èves futures by Jacques Baratier, 16 mins (co-prod. S.N. Pathé Cinéma).
  La Femme fleur by Jan Lenica, 11 mins (co-prod. Fior [Berlin]).
  Gloire à Félix Tournachon by M. Boschet and A. Martin, 20 mins (co-prod. Films M.B.).
  L'Invention de la photographie by M. Boschet and A. Martin, 21 mins (co-prod. F.M.).
  Mais où sont les nègres d'antan (Ex: *Les Nègres*) by A. Martin and M. Boschet, 21 mins (Co-prod. Films M. Boschet).
1965: *La Brûlure de mille soleils* by Pierre Kast, 24 mins.
  Les oiseaux sont des cons by Chaval, 3 mins.
  Le Passage by Cécile Decugis, 30 mins.
1966: *Europort* by Joris Ivens, 20 mins (co-prod. N.F.M. Rotterdam).
  Exils (*Divine comédie*) by Marc Scialom, 18 mins (co-prod. Service Recherches ORTF).
  Voilà l'ordre by Jacques Baratier, 46 mins (Co-prod. S.N. Pathé Cinéma).
1967: *Algérie, année zéro* by Jean-Pierre Sergent (and Marceline Loridan), 32 mins.
  Concerto pour un exil by Désiré Écaré, 30 mins (co-prod. Films de la Lagune).
  Les cow-boys sont noirs by Serge Henri Moati, 15 mins (co-prod. C.A.I.).
  Eden Miseria by Jacques Baratier, 20 mins.
  Le Retour d'un aventurier by Mustapha Alassane, 35 mins (co-prod. C.A.I.).
  Roméos et jupettes by Jacques Rozier, 8 mins.
  Sierra Falcon by Claude Barrois and Henry Capier, 16 mins.
1968: *Cabascabo* by Oumarou Ganda, 45 mins (co-prod. C.A.I.).
  Jeanne et la moto by Diourka Medveczky, 22 mins (co-prod. Films du Hibou).
  Noces de feu by Nicole Echard, 18 mins.

Piège by Jacques Baratier, 53 mins.

Pompo by Serge Henri Moati, 26 mins.

Prologue (Arrabal) by Jacques Baratier, 14 mins.

1969: *El Baston* (Ex: *Confusion*) by Nestor Almendros, 19 mins.

La Femme enceinte by Jean-Louis Comolli (co-prod. Films Xénia).

Femme noire, femme nue/A nous deux France by Désiré Écaré, 59 mins (co-prod. Films de la Lagune).

Impression soleil levant Pt. 1 by André S. Labarthe, 45 mins (co-prod. Universal).

Le Vieil Alkassa by Serge Henri Moati, 32 mins.

1970: *L'Afrique express* (Ex: *L'Afrique à vol d'oiseau*) by Danièle Tessier and Jacques Lang, 18 mins.

Bravo Zoulou by Danièle Tessier and Jacques Lang, 15 mins.

Chaval by Mario Ruspoli, 15 mins.

La Femme aux cent visages by Jean-Daniel Pollet, 10 mins.

Fleuves africains by Danièle Tessier and Jacques Lang (Co-prod. C.I.P.H.).

Impression soleil levant Pt. 2 by André S. Labarthe, 44 mins.

Israël et Ismaël by Henry Chapier, 18 mins.

Mort d'une girafe (Ex: *Une réserve africaine au Tchad*) by Danièle Tessier and Jacques Lang, 14 mins.

Tarra by Gilles Combet, 12 mins.

La Vallée fertile by Danièle Tessier and Jacques Lang, 22 mins (Co-prod. C.I.P.H.).

Le Wazzou polygame or *Le Mariage forcé* by Oumarou Ganda, 35 mins.

1971: *Jour de pluie* (*Hundertwassers Regentag*) by Peter Schamoni, 36 mins (Co-prod. P.S. Prod.).

1972: *Le Chavalanthrope* (Ex: *Journal d'un humoriste*) by Mario Ruspoli, 10 mins.

Combien de couleurs dans la main? (*Wieviel Farben hat die Hand?*) by Peter Schamoni, 30 mins.

Conte médiocre by Chaval, 7 mins.

1973: *Le Pays beau* by Michel Boschet and Georges Wolinski, 12 mins (co-prod. Films M.B.).

Une collection particulière by Walerian Borowczyk, 12 mins (Co-prod. P. Schamoni).

Vive la baleine by Mario Ruspoli and Chris Marker, 17 mins.

1974: *La Promenade* by Eddy Matalon, 9 mins.

1975: *Le Beau Samedi* by Renaud Walter, 26 mins.

L'Escargot de Vénus by Walerian Borowczyk, 5 mins.

O Gaule by Jean-Marie Goulet, 8 mins.

Un chant d'amour by Jean Genet, 26 mins.

La Véritable histoire de la bête du Gévaudan by W. Borowczyk, 18 mins.

1977: *L'Amour monstre de tous les temps* by Walerian Borowczyk, 15 mins.

1978: *Demain, la petite fille sera en retard à l'école* by Michel Boschet, 4 mins.

Insomnies (*Dorothea Tanning: Insomnia*) by Peter Schamoni, 15 mins (co-prod. P.S. Prod.).

Sine massacre Pt. 1 by Michel Boschet, 3 mins.

1980: *Le Petit Chaperon bleu, blanc, rouge* by Michel Boschet, 6 mins.

1981: *Elia Kazan outsider* by Annie Tresgot and Michel Ciment, 56 mins.

Junkopia by Chris Marker, 6 mins.

1984: *Scherzo infernal* by Walerian Borowczyk, 6 mins.

1986: *Sine massacre – Pt. 2* by Michel Boschet, 7 mins.

SHORT FILMS AWARDS (summary)

1950 *Fêtes galantes*: First Prize, Rio de Janeiro

1951 *L'Affaire Manet*: Best Biographical Documentary, Venice

1952 *Le Cœur d'amour épris du roi René*: Best Script, São Paulo

Images pour Debussy: Lumière Prize

Le Rideau cramoisi: Louis Delluc Prize; Special Mention by the Jury, Cannes.

1953 *Le Rideau cramoisi*: Fémina Prize; Merit Certificate, Edinburgh

1954 *Martin et Gaston*: Animation Prize, Venice; Golden Reel, Chicago

1955 *Le Voyage de Badabou*: Émile Cohl Prize (inaugural prize)

1956 *Nuit et brouillard*: Jean Vigo Prize; Grand Prix of French Cinema with Gold Medal

Dimanche à Pékin: First Prize, Tours

Paris, la nuit: Lumière Prize; Golden Bear, Berlin

1957 *Nuit et brouillard*: Best Documentary, Karlovy Vary

Dimanche à Pékin: Silver Medal, Moscow

Paris, la nuit: Bronze Medal, Moscow

Notre-Dame, cathédrale de Paris: Silver Medal, Moscow

La première nuit: Golden Ducat, Mannheim; Prize of the Film Societies, Cork

Barna Senese: Prize of the Catholic Television Days

La Joconde: First Prize, Tours

1958 *La Joconde*: Golden Palm, Cannes

Paris, la nuit: Golden Bear, Berlin

Les Hommes de la baleine: Best Documentary, Novisad (Yugoslavia); Best Documentary, Mar del Plata (Argentina)

1959 *Du côté de la Côte*: Best Tourist Film, Brussels; Certificate of Merit, Edinburgh

Images des mondes perdus: First Prize of the City of Paris

L'Horrible, bizarre et incroyable histoire de M. Tête: International Critics Prize, Tours

1960 *L'Horrible, bizarre et incroyable histoire de M. Tête*: Émile Cohl Prize

Les Astronautes: FIPRESCI Prize, Oberhausen; Prix du film de recherche, Venice; Special Prize and Gold Medal, Bergamo

Paris la belle: Special Jury Prize, Cannes

1961 *Les Inconnus de la terre*: International Critics Prize, Tours

1962   *Regard sur la folie*: Best Experimental Film, Bergamo; Diploma of Merit, Florence

1963   *La Jetée*: Golden Starship (First Prize), Trieste; Jean Vigo Prize; Golden Ducat, Mannheim; Gill Will Prize (Inaugural event)
M. Albert prophète: CIDALC Prize, Venice
A Valparaiso: FIPRESCI Prize, Mannheim; Special Prize, Leipzig; First Prize, Prades; Diploma of Merit, Bergamo

1964   *A Valparaiso*: FIPRESCI Prize, Oberhausen
La Femme fleur: Saint Mark's Lion, Venice; Bucranio d'argento, Padua
A: Best Short Film, Prades; Best Animated Film, Oberhausen
L'Invention de la photographie: Golden Mercury, Venice; First Prize, San Sebastian

1965   *Les oiseaux sont des cons*: Émile Cohl Prize
La Brûlure de mille soleils: Gold Medal, Trieste; Golden Louis, Locarno; Special Jury Prize, Rio de Janeiro; Gill Will Prize

1966   *Gloire à Félix Tournachon*: Special Prize, Cannes
Europort: Golden Ducat, Mannheim

1967   *Concerto pour un exil*: First Prize, Hyères; Special Jury Prize, Oberhausen
Sierra Falcon: Special Prize, Oberhausen

1968   *Cabascabo*: Special Jury Prize, Benalmadena; Special Jury Prize, Moscow
Pompo: Best Documentary, Dinard

1970   *Le Wazzou polygame*: Critics Prize, Dinard; First Prize, Ouagadougou

1972   *Le Chavalanthrope*: First Prize, San Sebastian

1973   *Le Pays beau*: 2nd Prize Animation, Oberhausen; Catholic Council's Prize, Oberhausen

1977   *L'Amour monstre de tous les temps*: Best Direction, Montreal

1980   *Insomnies*: Best Essay Film, Montreal

INDEX